Founders
and
Followers

CஐᏰᎲ

Movers and Shakers
Who Built Early Gouldsboro

on the Eastern Frontier

Lectures by the Reverend
Charles Austin Joy

Town of Gouldsboro Historical Society

GOULDSBORO · MAINE

Library of Congress Control Number 2020902573

ISBN   978-0-578-64961-0

Classification: DDC 974.145

Publisher: Town of Gouldsboro Historical Society
             P.O. Box 94
             Gouldsboro ME 04607

Website: www.gouldsborohistory.org

E-mail: gouldsborohistoricalsociety@gmail.com

In honored memory of

Ephraim Wales Taft
1795-1873

and

In loving memory of

Nathan Sargent Sargent
1870-1962

Town of Gouldsboro Historical Society's Board of Directors wishes to express sincere appreciation for the many members, donors, volunteers, Town Selectmen and officials, and other supporters over the years, whose accumulated devotion to the Society and our region's heritage has made it possible for us to publish this history of early Gouldsboro.

Jay Bricker   Beatrice Buckley   Marie Crawley

Anne Hopper   Sylvia Joy   Kenneth Kelly

Larry Newman   Larry Peterson   Andrew Somes

Jennifer Stucker   Colleen Wallace   Allen Workman

Contents

Foreword

This book is the first to tell the story of what went into the creation of a new community on the Schoodic Peninsula on the Eastern Frontier in Maine. For author Charles Joy, the founding of a frontier settlement becomes a tale of the many who ventured into the almost unknown; yet the story is peopled with flesh-and-blood actors whose plans, ambitions, and struggles for survival made it possible for a new town to overcome war and near-starvation to reach ultimate success as a vital part of the new state of Maine. And it is hearing and reading about these people's strivings in realistic, vivid detail that distinguishes speaker and author Charles Joy's presentation of this story. Some of the appeal of his talks derives from the brisk and entertaining delivery in a colorful and engaging style, reflecting his career as a preaching Episcopal priest. And much of his story's appeal is certainly due to the easy flow of carefully researched concrete specifics of life that make people of the 18th and 19th Centuries come alive for listeners and readers. But Charles Joy also shows a unique concern for the humanity of his subjects that brings his audience a distinctive understanding of how our past came to be. Along with this comes Joy's keen sense of the Maine heritage that is his own background, and in these essays on the early days of Gouldsboro, he conveys a strong sense of the land and of the engagement of the settlers with the unique rigors and promise of our downeast landscape.

This book is also a distillation of the work of the author, Charles Joy's longtime career as a Gouldsboro Historical Society speaker. Since the year 2000 his talks, covering a range of Maine cultural and historical topics from overviews of early Gouldsboro's economy to biographies of local figures, have always focused on individual people whose stories have made our region distinctive. The talks collected here form chapters almost all concerned with the founding and early history of settling the Schoodic region. The settlement was originally a plantation granted as Number Three, a privately owned township soon called Gouldsboro, on what was then a frontier on the eastern edge of the colonies that became the USA. The people who made this happen are always the focus of his presentations, and he has unearthed their stories through an astonishing amount of research scholarship in the archives of New England and beyond.

These chapters, slightly expanded essay examples of his talks as delivered, are a significant record of the author's long commitment to the Gouldsboro Historical Society and the town he loves. They reflect Joy's personal heritage as a descendant of local families, and show a close acquaintance with the historical complexities of family relationships here. But above all his talks have shown our audiences how carefully accumulated historical evidence gives documentary reliability to the colorful stories he has assembled. Each essay shows the author's extensive research, which is referenced through the listed sources (in abbreviated form) after every chapter. However because the essays derive from spoken delivery in the author's talks, they are not interrupted with specific footnotes at each quotation or cited fact; rather a careful look at the sources cited at the end of every chapter will show how and where the quotations and specifics are linked to their research origins. Because these talks were delivered over a period of many years, some later chapters restate issues developed in earlier ones; yet the result is a useful recapitulation of key issues, focusing on the most basic dimensions of the town's past.

For the Gouldsboro Historical Society the publication of these essays gives a special satisfaction for two reasons. First, it has been well over a century since any comprehensive historical work on early Gouldsboro has been published anywhere. The last and locally-known historical work of this kind in circulation has been *Historical Researches of Gouldsboro*, Grace Wood Clark's work of 1904, still kept in print by the Society. The time is truly overdue that a new work reflecting modern scholarship should be published, and Gouldsboro Historical Society is a most appropriate publisher to make it available to everyone interested in the Schoodic region's history. Second, bringing this work to publication is a concrete testimony that the Society continues to be committed to careful scholarly historical work about the Schoodic region. Of course the same commitment appears in several more of the Society's programs and publications, striving above all to bring interesting and reliable information about the region's heritage. And of course the Society's offerings also include a broad range of entertaining stories, folklore pieces, and other reflections of our culture that are part of our region's traditions. But it is fundamentally important that a historical society be able to show work at the highest standard of verifiable information of the region's background as it occurred, as free as possible of nostalgic hopes for what we might imagine our history to have been. With this book we hope to fulfill part of that obligation to present a careful and verifiable historical narrative.

Finally, this publication is offered in honor of a proud occasion for our town, being the bicentennial of the town's participation in the creation of Maine in 1820 as a new and separate state. That event over two hundred years ago was accomplished with considerable tension and conflict, nationally in the "Missouri Compromise," as well state-wide, and also within the new town itself. But in supporting independent statehood, our community seemed able to wrap up an important chapter in a continuing story that began for Gouldsboro townsmen with the early settlement that is so carefully described in this book. We hope the story is enjoyable for all who read it.

For the Town of Gouldsboro Historical Society:

Beatrice C. Buckley   *Anne Boyd Hopper*

Charlotte Sweeney   *Allen K. Workman*

GHS Publications Committee

Acknowledgments:

The Committee is most grateful to Wilfred E. Côté III for researching and furnishing the Founding Documents in Appendix B.

This book has benefited in its many illustrations made available through U.S. Government and Maine State Government sources such as the National Park Service, Department of the Interior, The Library of Congress, Smithsonian Institute, National Portrait Gallery, as well as through the Google Art Project, from Wikipedia, from Maine Historical Society, and from the courtesy of numerous museums. Photos from the Blance Archive of Gouldsboro Historical Society are courtesy of Mary Lou Hodge, GHS Curator.

For cover art the Committee is grateful to Oeno Gallery of Picton, Ontario.

Book design and cover design by Charlotte Sweeney.

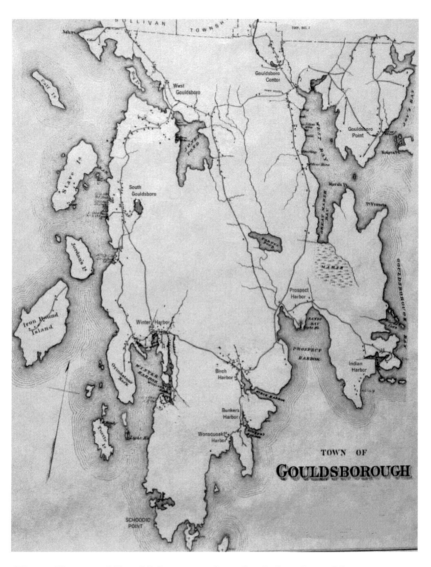

The villages of Gouldsboro as they had developed by 1881.
[Colby & Co, Ellsworth, 1881]

Preface

Many people have memories of history classes in high school or college, and these memories are often not positive. They experienced the study of history nakedly: lists of dates to be memorized, and as a result they have been turned off to the subject. Understandably so.

This common experience is a misapprehension. History is about people, of whatever era or place. Dates are simply a skeleton on which to hang the living reality of human beings in some earlier time. Although personalities from time past lived in worlds that looked and functioned very differently to ours, human beings are always people who share much with us in the experience of being human.

When I was a child I spent a good deal of time with older relatives who, like their families before them, lived in Gouldsboro and other small towns around Frenchman's Bay. I enjoyed hearing the oral traditions recounted by family members of life in an earlier and in many ways very different time. I became aware that the individuals who figured in these stories were connected to me not only by blood but also as members of the greater and ongoing human family. Their foibles and failings, their successes and triumphs, helped me understand myself and the world in which I was growing up.

In Gouldsboro I discovered some very early people who shared my name, but also many others whose names I had never heard and I began to wonder who these people were, what they had done, what part they had played in the ongoing saga of a familiar place. In such a way I became aware that dates were secondary to the study of human personalities and what their lives had accomplished. Some study led to the desire to know more, in the way that a detective story is scanned for connecting relationships or jigsaw puzzles challenge apparently disparate pieces to be fitted together in a pattern. Dates were only the filing labels for the real information. What I discovered was that this study of these early individuals helped me understand my own life and my place in the world's society. I became intrigued by the events and people who existed and functioned in this familiar place behind the living human memory.

These annual talks to the Gouldsboro Historical Society have attempted to portray personalities and events from an early period in Gouldsboro. In this way I have hoped to amplify contemporary understanding of this town and to bring to life, in some sense, people who, though long dead, were fully human and have been very much a part of the world and place we know.

Charles Austin Joy
Montpelier, Virginia
January 2020

Historical Introduction

From the point of view of Boston one reached the Maine settlements by sailing down the prevailing wind in an eastward direction as the coast extended; so the phrase "Down East" was developed early to refer to and describe the Province or District of Maine. Maine and its settlements were "the eastern lands" as viewed from the capital. Whatever lay farther east at any point along the Maine coast was "down", whatever was west toward New Hampshire and Boston was, from Maine's point of view, "up." But in whatever direction one looked, Boston and the Maine settlements were closely linked.

Massachusetts merchants had long looked hopefully to the eastward, toward the vast forested lands of the Territory of Sagadahoc newly won by the British the end of the Seven Years' War with France and her Indian allies. Mile after mile toward the sunrise stretched the lands of morning, mostly unsettled and empty of Europeans, but for time out of mind home of the Wabanaki Indians, "the people of the dawn." From pre-historic times Native Americans of the Algonquin language group – the ancestors of the Penobscots, Micmacs, Maliseets, and Passamaquoddies-- had inhabited the forests and coasts of eastern Maine. A huge and ancient shell-heap on the south shore of Jones's Cove in West Gouldsboro bears rich testimony to the ancient presence of the seasonally nomadic people in the area. By the 1760s the Native American population on the edge of the Schoodic region, ravaged by disease and war, had retreated to the heads of the Penobscot and Passamaquoddy Bays which bear their people's names.

As the Seven Years War was ending in 1762 with Britain's victory, one unresolved issue was the untouched and virgin land lying between Penobscot and St Croix Rivers, ceded by the French as a part of the settlement of peace. To whom would it be granted for settlement and administration? To Nova Scotia in the east which Britain had already received from France in 1713 and which had been settled as a British colony, or to Massachusetts in the west, whose territory in the District of Maine was contiguous to the lands of Sagadahoc in the Kennebec valley? Whichever way it was decided, to be valid the territory had to be assigned and confirmed by the British government in London in whose larger empire the disputed territories now lay.

Because Massachusetts merchants had had such a long background of war and settlement in the eastern lands, the story of Gouldsboro must begin in Boston, the financial and governmental capitol of the Province of Massachusetts Bay. There the legislature was seated that hired the surveyors who set off the newly acquired Maine lands in a grid of potential townships, issuing title to proprietors for settlement and development. In Boston as well were the three men who, as proprietors, would in different but complementary ways sire the Gouldsboro township.

The newly appointed Governor Bernard pressed the legislature in Massachusetts to seize the bull by the horns and to act in the matter. Relying on the belief that possession is nine tenths of the law, in February 1763 the General Court for Massachusetts granted to more than three hundred investors the lands east of the Penobscot River. These lands were to be surveyed into townships, each six miles square "to promote settlement to the eastward... between the river Penobscot and the river St Croix... on the seacoast, or on Penobscot or other rivers, to be located in a regular contiguous manner." Plans stipulated sixty Protestant families to be settled in each township within six years after the royal confirmation of the grants, and in each township three hundred acres were to be cleared for tillage, a meeting house to be erected and a minister settled. (See the founding documents detailing this in Appendix B.) There were to be two classes of these newly laid out townships: the six of the first class were to be surveyed between the Penobscot and the Union Rivers. These would become Bucksport, Orland, Penobscot, Sedgwick, Bluehill and Surry. The six townships of the second class were to lie to the east of Union River "in the vicinity of Mount Desert." These were: Number One [Trenton], Number Two [Sullivan], Number Three [Gouldsboro], Number Four [Steuben], Number Five [Harrington], and Number Six [Addison].

To Governor Bernard himself was awarded the great island called Mount Desert, ostensibly to offset and compensate for his large personal expenses in assuming the office of royal governor, in particular the costs of refurbishing the state apartments in Province House and Castle William in Boston. That altruism, however, cloaked a more pragmatic hope: that in order to confirm his own valuable personal gift Bernard would use the influence of his office to press the British government to award the disputed Sagadahoc territory to Massachusetts and not to Nova Scotia. Without waiting for full legal confirmation of the titles, Sir Francis Bernard had acted at once to begin development of his newly acquired island in Maine. Three surveying expeditions charted the area. Despite Bernard's best efforts, the project was slow in coming to its fruition, and it was not until December 1769 that the Privy Council decided in favor of the Massachusetts title.

Meanwhile, however, the development of the eastern lands was going forward through the labors of the proprietors to whom the newly laid out townships had been granted. The role of "proprietor" had been instituted early in New England history. Whereas the original use of the term had denoted the tenants of one single field, in 1692 it served in Massachusetts law to identify the owners of a town's undivided land. The emergence of this kind of proprietorship, holding large tracts of undeveloped land, was to have important implications for Gouldsboro into the nineteenth century and would have a significant impact on the story of its founding. The proprietorships of the plantation township designated as Number Three—Gouldsboro—were taken on by three men who are the subject of the opening chapters of this collection.

This book begins with the stories of these three proprietary founders—Nathan Jones, Robert Gould, and Francis Shaw. The next six chapters complete the story of those who followed—the other "movers and shakers"--great men and small who built the town of Gouldsboro as it grew and became ready to join the new state of Maine in 1820. The last chapter gives a telling snapshot of life in the town as it had developed by the mid -20th Century. All of these chapters originated as lectures given for the Gouldsboro Historical Society between 2000 and 2015.

--CAJ

Chapter 1

NATHAN JONES: QUARTER PROPRIETOR

Governor Francis Bernard, *patron of Nathan Jones. He employed Jones for early surveying of the Acadia and downeast region.*

This talk, given in August, 2003, was part of a series of presentations about the earliest founding of a plantation at Gouldsboro—originally known as "Township Number Three"—and its proprietors who brought the first English settlers into the area in the mid-1760s.

The grant by the Massachusetts legislature of Township Number Three—which became Gouldsboro-- was unusual in that only three men were named as Proprietors. Robert Gould provided money, Francis Shaw and his sons provided presence. They received three quarters of the township in undivided title. Nathan Jones, youngest of the three by a fair amount, received a quarter of Number Three in his own name and became resident at a very early stage. He is different from the other Boston-based proprietors in several interesting ways. His background was influential in forming his identity.

Nathan Jones was born 29 September 1734 in Weston, Massachusetts, a village very close to Boston. Whereas Gould and Shaw were city born and bred, Nathan Jones was brought up in an agricultural village. He was eldest child of Elisha Jones and his wife Mary Allen who had married in January of that year. Both of them were descended from old and prominent families, established there since the early Colonial period. Their length of residence in Weston is reflected in the Massachusetts tax list of 1771 when, for the town of Weston, there was a total of 177 tithables – that is, taxable men – and ten of them bore the name Jones. One of them was Elisha. He was the great formative figure in the life of his first born son, and to understand the father is to understand much about the son.

Elisha's valuation was not the highest but it was substantial. The land included twelve acres of pasture land, nine acres of tillage, fourteen acres of "English and upland mowing land," and fifteen acres of fresh meadow. The twenty nine acres of upland and meadow produced sixteen tons of hay a year to feed the ten cows and two horses through the long winters and late springs. For human consumption the land produced 100 bushels of grain and forty barrels of cider which in the English fashion would be fermented. Many deeds in the name of Elisha Jones record much dealing in land in Weston. At his death, Elisha's exact inventory in real estate was recorded, revealing a canny and substantial yeoman. House, barn and other buildings, £3000. The "Home Lott" of seventy acres, the most valuable parcel, £3010. The

A colonial-era home in Nathan Jones' home town of
Weston Mass. (The Samuel Train House, 1738)

"Allen farm" of sixty acres, £1820. "Nonesuch" farm of eighty acres, £1840. "Lott called Jerecho" of ninety acres, £800. Pasture and woodland "at Princeton," seventy acres, £1400. The estate thus totaled 370 acres valued at £11, 870.

Within the town of Weston Elisha Jones took a leading role. Residing in the First Precinct, he was precinct clerk and auditor of the precinct accounts. He served as moderator of town meetings, was town treasurer and assessor and selectman. He was part of committees for the schoolhouse and the workhouse and Justice of the Peace. He represented Weston in setting boundaries with Sudbury and Natick, was overseer of highways, and overseer of the poor. As a member of the First Parish Church, his was the second pew east of the pulpit. He served the church in looking after meetinghouse repair, layings out and assigning pews, and procurings supplies for the minister's ordination.

Elisha's public service involved membership in the General Court, the governing body of the colony. This service, as well as his conservative political position, threw him into close contact with Sir Francis Bernard, the royal governor, and with those in the governor's circle of friends and associates. Sir Francis was given Mount Desert Island in the division of eastern Maine, bringing that area to prominent awareness.

Land was in the Joneses' blood; it was the key to their prosperity. In 1734, the year of his eldest son Nathan's birth, Elisha received from his siblings "in consideration of several sums of money" the "Mansion House and home of late belonging to our said father, and all lands and estates both real and personal." Even beyond the boundaries of his native town, he was involved in land development in western Massachusetts where, in 1762, Nathan himself – at the age of twenty eight – was one of the purchasers of East Hoosuck (now Adams). When in 1764 the legislature gave grants in twelve new eastern Maine Townships, Elisha was a grantee among a large group of proprietors of "all that Tract of Land lying among a large Territory of Sagadahock on the East side of Mount-desert River now called Union River"—a section of modern-day Ellsworth.

When these twelve townships were laid out in preparation for granting and settlement, Nathan Jones and a surveyor called Frye were "employed in Surveying those Towns," appointed by resolve of the General Court in January 1764. In advancing age he would recall the exploits of his young manhood in the uncharted wilderness of eastern Maine that would become his home.

". . . in the year seventeen hundred and sixty four I was employed by Sir Francis Bernard then Governor of the Province of Massachusetts Bay as commander of a party employed to explore the woods and view the rivers and bays particularly that of Passamaquoddi in the eastern parts of said Province . . . and to perform a survey thereof. . . we proceeded . . . in our surveys and agreeable thereto in August following made return of our doings

A grandiose summer mansion for a Royal Governor of Massachusetts, --- Governor Barnard's predecessor William Shirley who served until 1757—shown here as it survived in the 20th century Boston area. [U.S. Library of Congress]

to the said Governor Barnard." The date of the letter was 1785, when Nathan Jones was fifty one and royal governors were no more.

Thus, through his prominent father Elisha, Nathan Jones was connected to the Royal Governor in his interests in eastern Maine – the golden bond. He first travelled to Mount Desert Island with Governor Bernard, to whom the island had been granted, as his surveyor in 1762. In this way he became familiar with the Gouldsboro peninsula. Thus, when Number Three came to be granted to three men, uniquely among the twelve townships, Nathan Jones was one of those on whom it was bestowed (see Appendix B). As surveyor with a strong link to governmental power, Nathan Jones claimed one quarter of the township as his own, including the cove and pond that even today bear his name. By 1766 he was living in Gouldsboro. He had married in 1756 Sarah Seaverns, also and predictably of Weston. They became the parents of twelve children. The first five – Nahum, Sarah, Theodore, Louisa and Pamela – were born in Weston, the last of these in 1763. The next child, son Abijah, was born in April 1765 in Gouldsboro—now a native to a part of eastern Maine that a decade earlier had been entirely French.

A Royal Governor's grand staircase in the Boston summer mansion of Governor Bernard's 1757 predecessor, William Shirley. [U.S. Library of Congress]

By 1778 the Revolutionary War, begun three years earlier at Lexington and Concord, had taken a severe toll on the Jones family and on Gouldsboro. Among the casualties of war, Colonel Elisha Jones, friend of royal governors and Loyalist to the last, left Weston and all his property for British occupied Boston. "[He] fled to Enemies of the

United States for protection & never returned to his habitation," said a later chronicler. He died there in the winter of 1775 and was buried from Trinity Church.

The war's effects were especially profound in Down East Maine where the infant lumber economy, totally dependent on shipping to Boston for a market, was interrupted by vessels of the Royal Navy. The basic way of life and survival were threatened. The inhabitants of Gouldsboro petitioned the General Court in Boston for relief in May 1778. The petition described what had become "a Deplorable Situation occasioned by the total Stagnation of the Lumber Trade, upon which we mostly depended for a Living, and the frequent Allarms whereby we was obliged to March to Machias last year Intirely prevented us from Raising and Provisions. . .or procureing Hay for our Cattle. . . ."

In October of that year the House of Representatives in Boston received a lengthy petition from Gouldsboro which stated that "in the course of the last four years [they] have been perplexed with Numbers of litigious complaints and information Against Col Nathan Jones of Gouldsboro wherein he has been represented as an Enemy to the Liberties of this Country." After detailed discussion, thirty townsmen affirmed that "we have found him under all his difficulties a Peaceable and useful member of society a friend to Order & Regulation ready & willing to comply with the present mode of government, & to supply the wants & necessities of poor people, besides supplying prisoners on their way from Hallifax Gaol [jail] on free cost, and feeding the Militia . . . Add to these his service in the coarse of two Years as one of the Committee of Correspondance Inspection & Safety in the township of Gouldsborough wherein he has served to the universal satisfaction of Evry inhabitant." From neighboring New Bristol, Number Two [Sullivan] came a similar testimony "We . . . his Neighbours . . . look on such Accusations to be Groundless, & that We have not the least fear from any Information he will give against the Country. . . ."

In later years, Jones's fascination with the land and its development, so like his father's interests, continued. In a contract of 1788 with the Committee for the Sale of Lands in the County of Lincoln, he "agrees to Survey a Road from Union River to the plains on the East Side of Narraguagus River . . . to Form a good Road," the road to run on an eastward bearing. He is to employ a surveyor, and to maintain "a field Book of Remarks, for all which services, on his making a Return of his doings," he is to be paid "in Lands thirty two shillings for each & every working Day that he and his party may be employed therein." The report of the work was submitted on New Year's Eve 1790 dated at "Goldsboro'." The great difficulty of laying out this road through the raw wilderness is reflected in his report. "After passing Taunton Bay, I found it impossible to carry the Road to the Northward of Schooduck Mountain by reason of continued Hills, Ledges and Lakes. I therefore run to the Southward of that Mountain making as straight a Course as will be found convenient for a Road, until I came out of Gouldsboroughs Bay, in the Township of No. 4 [Steuben] from whence the County of Washington have laid out a road to Machias." His recommendation was to connect the proposed route to the existing Washington County road "which is the most eligible for the great Post road."

Having surveyed and explored the land, he submitted as well "an estimate of the expense of clearing a Road through, and as it is in my power to avail myself of advantages which others have not, I flatter myself that I can accomplish it on terms more advantageous to Government than any other." His proposal reveals some of what was involved is creating roads where none had been before. "I will undertake to clear a Road from Union River to the bounds of No. 4 to bridge all the Brooks, and cut the Trees close to the Ground, Twenty feet wide, for Twenty Five Dollars pr mile and in proportion, if it is thought necessary to be mostly paid in Land; and as I am persuaded that I have seen the Price of the work lower than any other can do, I

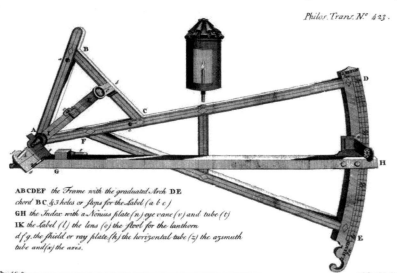

Philos. Trans. N° 423.

ABCDEF *the Frame with the graduated Arch* **DE**
chord **BC** *& 3 holes or stops for the Label (a b c)*
GH *the Index with a Nonius plate (n) eye vane (v) and tube (t)*
IK *the Label (l) the lens (o) the stool for the lanthorn*
d f g. the shield or ray plate (h) the horizontal tube (z) the azimuth tube and (x) the axis.

A surveyor's level and quadrant of Governor Bernard's era.
[Library of Congress: Drawing of Elton's Quadrant.
From "Philosophical Transactions of the Royal Society," 1731-1732.]

shall expect that the price of the Lands will be as low as any that has been sold by Government in this County."

In the 1790s, throughout the tumult of quieting or confirming settlers' land titles, and the massive sale to William Bingham of the Shaw/Gould section of Gouldsboro (see Chapter 5), Nathan Jones continued to live prosperously and peacefully in his Quarter. In 1796 he was described as "the richest character to the east of Penobscot, owning "the best part" of Gouldsboro. " He has . . . a large farm, good house, and three mills, which go by water from a pond above him which he lets through by sluices. He has been making experiments of all kinds and is useful to the country." Lord Ashburton, who was writing the description, goes on to note that Nathan Jones was "an artful [crafty, tricky] man, having resided long in Maine, has picked up several other of the most valuable spots, and I believe has been cheating his neighbors, especially the former proprietors of Gouldsboro' but for that there is no remedy and we can only take care of ourselves. He owns several vessels at sea, which he builds himself at his wharf; while we were there one of his ships returned from Europe on freight for her first voyage, which had entirely paid her cost." Like many wealthy people his assets were largely invested, mostly in land, so he experienced some tightness for ready cash as the Eighteenth Century ended and the new country was getting organized.

His residence was a ten room, probably two story, "Mansion house" built facing south across his wharf and mills at the head of Jones's Cove. A selection of items in his estate inventory reveal something of his way of life. In the keeping room were a clock, a mahogany dining table around which were Windsor chairs, on a carpet. A spy glass was also in evidence, by which he could watch his returning ships clearing Hog Island at the entrance to Jones's Cove. The best bedroom, probably the master bedchamber, was heated by a fireplace near which were a round mahogany table and an easy chair, a desk and bookcase as well as the bedstead. Among the books were listed "old Bible," "Common prayer book," Sullivan's *History of Maine*, *The Shipmaster's Assistant,* and intriguingly, "other books on the desk." The "little bedroom" had only a bed and chair. In the "North room" was a Dutch liquor case with its blown bottles, an "electorising machine," a powder canister for a muzzle loading gun, and two half gallon bottles and a demijohn, probably containing rum. The "north chamber" held a curtained bedstead, two square tables, a stand, six chairs, a mirror and a warming pan for icy winter nights. Four more bedchambers, sparsely furnished, only two of which had beds, and a bed and chest of drawers in a third. The kitchen, heart of a house in the New England climate and the focus of the work of Sarah Jones, was furnished more fully than other rooms. Included were cooking vessels, a "washing machine," cheese tub and cheese press, loom and spinning wheel, some silver, some blue and white cups and saucers, and a sidesaddle and saddle when Colonel and Mrs Jones travelled by horseback.

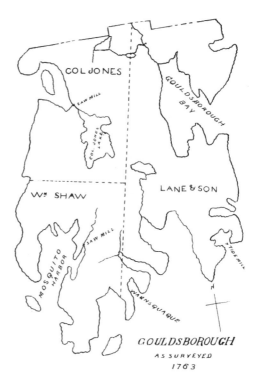

Gouldsboro map of 1764 showing the northwest quadrant owned by Nathan Jones.
[Gouldsboro Historical Society]

His well stocked farm included as livestock three yoke of oxen, twenty five cows and three horses, forty three lambs and sheep, six hogs and poultry. Carts and sleds, a gondala ["heavy flat bottomed barge, used in New England"], blacksmith equipment and carpenter's tools, reflect the many activities of his daily life..

In his massive real estate holdings were included 5800 acres in Jones's Quarter in addition to Stave and Hog Islands in Gouldsboro; 100 acres on Great Duck Island; 5300 acres in Trenton; and a mill with 100 acres at Morancy in Sullivan.

Nathan Jones was a country man and, as farmers had by necessity to be, a remarkably able man in many areas. He was surveyor, builder and sailor of ships, farmer, carpenter and blacksmith. He owned a brick kiln on Jones's Cove, as well as saw mills and a grist mill. He served as Justice of the Peace, and as agent of government.

He died at his residence on 7 May 1806 in his seventy first year, the last and youngest of the three original Proprietors. His life had not been without its sadnesses. His eldest son Nahum Jones, "for some years merchant in St John's, New Brunswick" died in 1793, aged thirty five, at St Martin's. His namesake, young Nathan, aged twenty two, "drowned when a small sail boat overset in Frenchman's Bay" in late autumn 1789. Nathan Jones's inventory was taken on 24 June, when one of those appointed for that task was Thomas Hill, his old neighbor in Weston and for many years his near neighbor in Gouldsboro at Jones's Quarter. His will had been written the previous autumn, in September 1805. Perhaps already failing in health, Nathan Jones made distribution of his property since he was "advanced in life and knowing the uncertainty of it, and being persuaded of the duty incumbent on all who are blest with any property to make such distribution of it as may best prompt the happiness of those who are to enjoy it after us." Besides the divisions of his estate among his children, he made provision for Bluehill Academy "as a small tribute of respect for those who initiated this establishment and as a pledge of my best wishes for its success." He expressed his rationale: "I have considered the establishment and support of literary institutions unitedly with religion as the source from whence must flow all the order and happiness of civil society."

One final little twist of history. In the Vital Records of Weston, Massachusetts on page 132, two entries stand side by side. "Rev'd mr Asa Dunbar of Salem & Miss Mary Jones of Weston Joyned in marriage pr Revd Mr Samull Woodward minister of the Gospel in Weston Octr 22 1772." Immediately follows "Thomas Hill & Rebecca Train Both of Weston Were Joyned in marriage pr the Revd mr Samull Woodward minister of the Gospel in Weston Octr 29 1772." These two unions, one week apart, would show interesting connections.

Thomas and Rebecca Hill would remove to Gouldsboro onto land purchased from Nathan Jones. Mrs Asa Dunbar (nee Mary Jones) was younger sister of Nathan Jones. Among her children was Cynthia Dunbar (1787-1872). She would marry a man who owned a pencil factory and made pencils in Concord, Massachusetts. His name was John Thoreau (1787-1858) and they would produce, among their children, a son whose name was Henry David Thoreau (1817-1862). He would become the famous and eccentric naturalist and author of *Walden* and *On the Duty of Civil Disobedience*. His great uncle was Nathan Jones, quarter Proprietor of Gouldsboro.

Sources

*James S. Leamon, *Revolution Downeast: The War for American Independence in Maine,* 1993

*John Howard Ahlin, *Maine Rubicon: Downeast Settlers during the American Revolution,* 1966.

Bangor Historical Magazine

*Muriel Sampson Johnson, *Early Families of Gouldsboro, Maine,* 1990.

*Grace Wood Clark, *Historical Researches of Gouldsboro, Maine.* 1904.

William Bingham, Maine Lands (ed. Frederick Allis)

Maine Families in 1790, Vol. II.

Documentary History of the State of Maine.

*Massachusetts Archives, Eastern Lands Papers.

*Hancock County Deeds and Probate

*Middlesex County, Massachusetts, Deeds and Probate

*Vital Records of Weston, Middlesex County, Massachusetts

*Massachusetts *Chronicle*
.

A restoration small open schooner of the type used by early settlers on the Eastern Frontier. This workboat and fishing vessel would be the type Jones used to survey the downeast coast.

[The restoration "Chebacco" boat, the "Lewis H. Story"—Essex Shipbuilding Museum, Essex MA]

Chapter 2

"WHAT'S IN A NAME?"
ROBERT GOULD
AND HIS TOWN

The church of Robert Gould and his family in Boston--Christ Church, or "Old North Church" of Paul Revere fame, as shown in a 1880s engraving.

This talk on the man for whom Gouldsboro was named was given in August of 2001. It introduces an important dimension of the plantation's founding--its crucial reliance on funding from Boston merchants.

శ

Plants begin with seeds. So do plantations. In the case of the settlement plantation called Gouldsboro, that infant seedling on the far eastern coast of Massachusetts grew from seeds promulgated by moneyed commercial interests centered in Boston. This eastern territory had been newly gained by the victory of Great Britain over France in the recently concluded Seven Years War. Its new opportunities for investment were seized upon in older Massachusetts, where Boston was the financial as well as the political center of the colony. Its merchant community spied new and promising ground for economic development.

On 27 January 1764, "in the Fourth Year of the Reign of his Majesty George the Third," the legislature of Massachusetts Bay confirmed for settlement the grant of six plantations, called "townships," lying east of Union River in the territory Great Britain had recently received from France in the Peace of Paris. (See the Historical Introduction and Appendix B.) A grid on the coastal area was made by surveyors in blocks six miles square individually, and each numbered.

Much later, in February 1789, Township Three of these six township plantations was officially incorporated to become a self-governing Town under the name of Gouldsborough. Its name was now officially received. Next door was Number Two, called unofficially "New Bristol" and "Frenchman's Bay," before it received its incorporated name of Sullivan. Number Four bordering Gouldsboro on the east was known in that title until its incorporation as Steuben in 1795. It was only at incorporation along with town self-government that names became officially ascribed. Yet at a much early time a name had been attached to Number Three. On 14 July 1766, for example, Boston merchant John Rowe noted: "Mr Nathan Jones arriv'd from Goldsberough this morning." This diary entry reveals what was apparently the early pronunciation of the name. The long usage of that name, found years before incorporation, is significant. Thus arises the question, who is the person, clearly of importance, behind the name used for the incipient settlement in eastern Maine?

The reference is to the subtle but unusually powerful influence of one man, Robert Gould, one of the three patentees with Nathan Jones and Francis Shaw. But why Gould? Why not Shawsborough or Jonesborough? A further sign of the importance of Robert Gould is reflected in the constant use of his name as Robert Gould Shaw, in the family of another patentee unrelated by blood. Extensive research still leaves many questions and much mystery about this interesting, sad, enigmatic man who is clearly terribly important in Gouldsboro's story. There is no portrait of him, no collection of private papers. Some sense of his identity and importance must be derived from public archives.

Robert Gould was born about 1719 in a place and of parentage so far unidentified. Though his parentage is undetermined, clearly of first importance in his development was his uncle John Gould, a figure of some stature in Boston. To understand something of the uncle is to understand much about the nephew.

John Gould was born in 1699, only twenty years older than nephew Robert. . As an adult he became prominent in the merchant community in Boston, which provided the basis of the town's economic life. John Gould was a man of parts and property. Deeds record many transactions in land; he owned a distilling house; he grew silkworms; he owned a warehouse on Town Dock.

It is a matter of some interest that the three proprietors of Gouldsboro were not Puritans. Each had close connections with the Anglican church in Boston. Robert Gould, like Uncle John, was a devout Anglican. With nephew Robert and the royal governor Francis Bernard, John Gould was a founder of the Anglican Society in the city in 1758. Its purpose was for the relief and aid of "Many Persons . . . in very good circumstances [who] are by the Providence of God reduced to so great necessities as to need Charity. . . ." John Gould was one of the wardens of Christ Church, now known as "Old North Church" of Paul Revere fame. In 1744 its peal of six bells, one of only three peals in the colonies, was cast in England. Inscribed on one bell are the words "the first ring of bells cast for the British Empire in North America, John Gould, Church Warden." In addition to Christ Church, John Gould owned pew 74 in King's Chapel, the chapel royal in Boston, where he would be buried at the left of the center aisle.

His surviving children, first cousins to Robert Gould, were Loyalists in the Revolution. Among them was son William who came to a tragic end in 1784, "found dead in the cellar in Roxbury; he fell downstairs and his cane was forced through the back of his mouth causing death." John Gould's daughter Sarah was his chief heir. She was married to the Reverend John Troutbeck, Anglican priest in

Boston at King's Chapel for twenty years, from 1755 to 1775 when they returned to England at the outbreak of revolution. Sarah Troutbeck inherited massively from her father's estate, living after the death of her husband at Dacre in Cumberland. In old age she returned to Massachusetts, dying at Hingham in 1813 at the age of 77. Her descendants remaining in England were graduates of Oxford University and Anglican priests.

The parlor/ dining room of a merchant's house in Gould's era. [National Park Service- Salem Maritime National Historic Site]

Uncle John was on death's doorstep when he made his will, dated 28 December 1771. He died on January 8, 1772 in his 72nd year. The Reverend Mather Byles, who inherited ten Pounds under John's will, preached the funeral sermon, in which he commended him as "one of the most valued and respected members" of Christ Church. "I never visited him without improvement; I never left him without regret." He further observed "with what constancy and exemplary devotion he attended all the solemn offices of the church." High secular praise was accorded him as well. He was "well known for his extensive Trade, and great Integrity and . . . for fulfilling all his Engagements with the most nice and scrupulous exactness." Such was the role model and mentor of Robert Gould.

At the age of thirty one, on 4 February 1750, Robert Gould married Elizabeth Nelson. They became the parents of three daughters: Elizabeth ("Betty"), Sarah ("Sally") and Hannah. All three were baptized in Trinity Church, where also Gould's black servant boy Quaco was baptized in 1769.

It is fascinating to read from Probate records the detailed inventory and description of the family house. The furnishings provide insight into the texture and quality of the life of the Goulds, an intricate picture of the family who inhabited the house. It is as close as we can come to knowing this cultivated and prosperous man, through these rich concrete images selected from the total inventory. Built of brick in Back Street in the prosperous north end of Boston, the house always belonged to Uncle John as well as several other tracts in the same street which he had accumulated from 1739 onward.. Robert's store, Christ Church and the Mill Pond were all close by. It was only a few streets away from North Square where were the residences of the Shaws and of Paul Revere (see Chapter Three). The family home of Robert and Elizabeth Gould was ample, and had eleven rooms, with a garret at the top.

Merchant's bed chamber in Gould's era — (the 1762 Derby House in Salem Mass.)

[National Park Service- Salem Maritime National Historic Site]

On the main floor were a "front room," parlor [dining room], large kitchen and back sitting room. The front room appears to have been a comfortable place of entertainment. Here were a mahogany card table, two tea tables, silver tea kettle and stand, and silver coffee pot and stand. There were four windows providing abundant natural light. These had damask curtains for winter and red and white check for the summer season. Six side chairs with damask seats, two mahogany arm chairs and a mahogany settee provided abundant

32

seating for guests. Decoration was completed by two flower pots for spring and summer use, two sconce looking glasses and a pair of branched candlesticks, probably also in silver. The floor was covered with a single large carpet and three strips of Wilton carpet. A fireplace with brass andirons and equipment provided heat in cold weather.

The center piece of the parlor/dining room was a square mahogany dining table with six mahogany chairs upholstered in leather and two "round chairs" [corner chairs] with wooden seats. An eight day clock ticked away the time. "Scotch carpet" covered the floor as well as a painted floor cloth of canvas. On the walls seven "pictures under glass" were probably engravings and were lit by a pair of "plated candlesticks." Among the dishes for dining were blue and white china, cream ware, clear glass, and two blue and white tea pots. Eleven blown decanters for wine and spirits, a tea chest and a sugar chest completed the furnishings. The three windows in the parlor sported two sets of curtains: one in yellow fabric and a second set in fabric that matched the furniture upholstery.

The back sitting room, where apparently the family gathered in daily life, held another mahogany dining table and a maple table, perhaps for serving, covered with a painted cloth, (a kind of oilcloth). A globe lamp provided light. Thirteen pictures under glass and a looking glass on the walls provided decoration. Daily meals were served in "sundry cooking & glass ware." The floor was covered with "an old painted floor cloth." Eight leather-bottom chairs and an old couch gave seating space. For the master of the house, a mahogany desk served a useful purpose, as well as "1 old fashioned" desk and bookcase (today called most commonly a "secretary.") Books in the bookcase represented Robert Gould's interests in religion and business. Five Bibles and a Book of Common Prayer, perhaps used for daily prayers, served a family who owned a pew in Trinity Church. Hebrew religion was represented by Josephus's *History of the Jews*, and the *Life of King David*. Anglican theology and worship appeared in the *Works of Bishop Beveridge* , William Law's popular *Whole Duty of Man*, and Bishop Sherlock *On Death*. Personal devotion appeared in Nelson's *Feasts and Fasts of the Church of England* and Thomas a Kempis's *Imitation of Christ*. Robert Gould the merchant and man of business included in his library *The History of New England*, a volume entitled *Surgery*, and *Money on Interest*, as well as a gazetteer. On intriguing entry lists "13 old books on various subjects." One wonders how old and on what subjects.

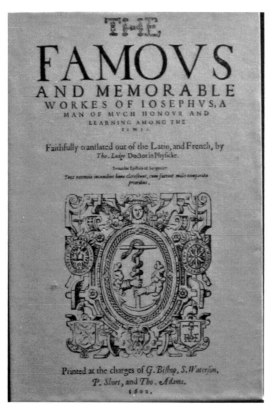

Title page from a book edition like the one in Gould's inventory—Josephus' History of the Jews. [The Diaspora Museum, Tel Aviv]

The "large kitchen" predictably included vessels of iron, copper, bell metal, brass and pewter, probably mostly cooking equipment. The large pine table and surrounding room were lit by six iron candlesticks and "green handle" knives and forks to accompany "everyday dishes."

On the second floor, the "front chamber" held a mahogany four poster bed with two quilts, one of red bordered calico and one in blue and white fabric. The bed curtains and the window curtains, were of blue and white chintz. Extra dishes were stored in the closet of the room.

The "2nd chamber" was apparently the master bedroom of Robert and Elizabeth Gould. Two windows lit the space with daylight. A looking glass and a dressing glass, another secretary desk, and a mahogany chest of drawers were among the furnishings. An elaborate bedstead was composed of a feather bed, bolster and pillows, and a trundle underneath for a child. Six pictures under glass hung on the bedroom walls. A fireplace provided winter heat. The floor was covered with "2 Scotch carpets" and seven Wilton carpets. Here in this inner sanctum of the master and mistress of the house were kept the "silver knifes & forks," as well as house linen consisting of table cloths, breakfast cloths, towels and sheets.

Also in this room, and perhaps in some ways most fascinating of all, was Robert Gould's rather colorful wardrobe. Four "dark" suits in blue, gray, black and light gold provided variety. Four jackets in blue silk knit, cloth of gold, velvet, and black silk ("with breeches") were augmented by breeches and waistcoat of "spotted jean," striped linen waistcoats and striped trousers. Two cloaks, one scarlet and one dark, as well as a beaver hat and a walking cane were used for outside wear. Basic clothing included shirts, cravats and stocks, hose in silk and worsted. Yarn and thread were provided for repairs. Public dress was completed by silk gloves and handkerchiefs, gold sleeve buttons, knee buckles, and a "pinch back watch." For the end of the day were twenty nightcaps.

A gentleman's waistcoat for an 18th Century Massachusetts merchant [National Park Service-Salem Maritime National Historic Site]

A "vendue room" and adjoining chamber held nine maps and another clock, among other odds and ends of furnishings. In the garret (doubtless under lock and key) was a breathtaking array of silver probably taken downstairs to the parlor for special dinners: a tankard, a can, a two handled cup, tea pot, a pair of butter boats, a pair of salt cellars, a castor, punch strainer, punch ladle, soup ladle, twenty five table spoons, tea spoons, a tea strainer and sugar tongs.

Other inventoried possessions included --typically for a colonial merchant-- a black slave couple Charles and Phoebe, the pew in Trinity Church, a horse and chaise, and one "fiddle & case." His neighbor Francis Shaw Jr also had a violin. One wonders if he and Robert Gould played together, perhaps the contemporary music of Scarlatti, Mozart and Paganini.

The man in his personal setting is intimately revealed in his home, but it is as Robert Gould the merchant that the investment in Gouldsboro must be seen. Nephew Robert was in business with Uncle John. The store was in Back Street not far from the house, opposite the tavern called "Crown and Sceptre," near the Mill Bridge. The inventory of the store is indicated in part by an advertisement that appeared in autumn 1762, when a variety of goods had been imported from Bristol in the ship *Betsy and Ruth.* Hardware was prominent. Pewter, lead, shot and window glass window glass were included, as well as painters' supplies. These included linseed oil, brushes, Spanish brown, stone and ochre colors, and white lead to form the basis of paint.

A merchant ship at an 18th Century Massachusetts wharf—(1797 East India ship in Salem Mass.) [National Park Service- Salem Maritime National Historic Site]

Dishes also were included in the shipment. Blue and while Delft, perhaps like similar china in Robert's parlor, yellow ware and flint glassware (crystal) were being offered for sale. Also included were English beer from Bristol and Dorsetshire, and Welch ale, like that which Robert drank with fellow merchant and friend John Rowe after a dinner party in May 1766. In addition to these goods, he advertised in 1766 the sale of rice, snuff, beaver fur, Muscavado [brown] sugar, spices cinnamon, nutmeg, mace and cloves, as well as tea and coffee.

Robert Gould was on his own following the death of Uncle John just after New Year's Day in 1772. He then advertised his reopened store "on Back Street leading to Charlestown Ferry. . . where he delights taking in all kinds of merchandise to sell for ready money only on Commission." Besides the store, he ran a pearling works beside the Charlestown Ferry where potash was produced to make soft soap. He ran as well an auction house where in January 1775 he sold "by Public Vendue" cloth goods from England and Ireland, silver, writing paper, knives in cases and other cutlery. "A large & valuable collection of books both new and second hand" included works in "Divinity, History, Philosophy, Physic, Mathematics, Astronomy, Arithmetic, Novels, Plays" and "one elegant sett of Patrick Lowths, and Whitby on the Old & New Testament." He also held auctions abroad in the city, as when, in February 1775, he sold all the household goods at the residence of Mr William Graves "a few doors north of Hancock's Wharf." At Robert Gould's death his shop, as one might expect, was well and variously stocked: buttons of all kinds, snuff boxes, razors, shoe buckles, clothing, dishes, soap, many bolts of fabrics of all kinds including "60 yds widows crape." Even a Jew's Harp and Dutch spectacles were among the goods.

The financial backing for the development of the infant settlement in Number Three was deeply grounded in the intricacy of the trading connections between Boston and London. Therefore the coming of the war with Britain had profound effect on the economic underpinning of Boston and, by extension, of Gouldsboro. The vast and intricate interconnection of trade in supply and demand, based largely on credit, was ruptured. Among the casualties was Robert Gould. Despite the diversity of his business, his most massive investment was in support of the development of Gouldsboro with Nathan Jones and Francis Shaw. It was a very huge expense but with very little overt success. Gould's business affairs at his death were in shambles. He left no will. He was heavily indebted to the English mercantile houses of Reeve and Devonshire in Bristol, and to Lane & Son and Thomas Fraser in London, to whom he had mortgaged Gouldsboro township in 1769. By 1771, sixty three families had settled in Gouldsboro. The overhead costs to the three partners amounted to 123,411 pounds sterling, 411 shillings and 6 pence – a fortune of debt. That sum was calculated "exclusive of time and trouble for 9 years past."

Misfortune appeared to stalk the family. Gould himself suffered for years from gout, at least since 1766. This adds understanding to the use of the walking stick listed among his effects. Elizabeth his wife died on 23 February 1776. Less than a year later Merchant Robert followed "after a few days' illness." Both were buried from Trinity Church. His daughters Sarah and Hannah died unmarried. The third daughter Elizabeth had married John Baker Brimmer in 1770 and by him she had one child, Elizabeth, born in 1771, who died aged twelve in August 1783. John Baker Brimmer died at the age of thirty eight in June 1784, and Elizabeth Gould Brimmer died in September 1793, aged 42. The elegant house in Back Street which had actually belonged to Uncle John passed to John Gould's daughter Sarah Troutbeck and was sold. Robert Gould's company was bankrupt. Because he had apparently given a financial start to Francis Shaw, the name Robert Gould was carried in several generations of that family, but no one of his own blood survived. His name lives on in Gouldsboro, Hancock County, Maine.

Sources

*Acts and Resolves of Massachusetts Bay, Vol. 17 (1761-1764).
*Historical Researches of Gouldsboro Maine, Grace Wood Clark, 1904.
*Files of Boston Gazette.
*Boston: A Topographical History. Walter Muir Whitehill, 1963.
*King and People in Provincial Massachusetts. Richard L. Bushman, 1985.
*Records of Trinity Church, (ed.) Oliver and Peabody in Publications of Colonial Society of Massachusetts, 1980.
*Annals of King's Chapel, Henry Wilder Foote. Vol II, 1896.
*Records of Christ Church, Boston.
*The Colonial Clergy and the Colonial Churches of New England, Frederick Lewis Weis, 1936.
*Biographical Sketches of Loyalists of the American Revolution, Gregory Palmer, 1984.
*Letters and Diary of John Rowe, (ed.) Anne Rowe Cunningham, 1903.
*Suffolk County, Massachusetts, Probate, Dockets 15077 and 16129.
*Suffolk County Deeds.

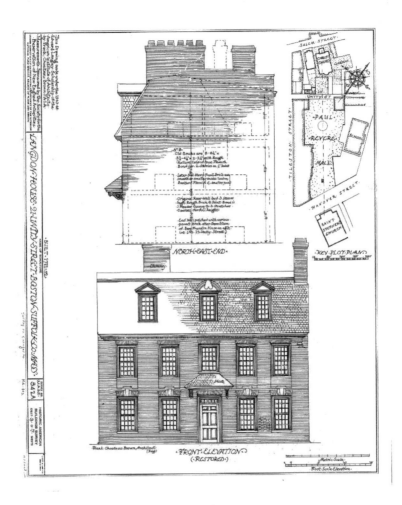

A Boston merchant's house of 1713.

[The Langdon House, Boston: US Park Service]

Chapter 3

FRANCIS AND THE SHAWS

Samuel Shaw, Francis Shaw senior's younger son and brother of the Gouldsboro colonist, as he appeared in the frontispiece as author of his own published journals. Samuel was on the staff of Revolutionary General Knox and the first American consul in Canton, China.

This talk on the founding Shaw family was delivered at the Old Town House in Gouldsboro in August of 2000. While the talk expands on how Boston capital struggled to support the new settlement, it also shows how heavily absorbed was this founding family in shaping Gouldsboro's early development.

ℰ

Without Boston there would be no Gouldsboro story as we know it. The city is the seedbed out of which the infant plantation in Number Three – Gouldsborough (as spelled then) ‑came to life. Boston to us is a distant city up in Massachusetts, but it is impossible fully to consider or understand the foundations of Number Three on the then distant frontier without some picture of Boston where the holders of the original title to the settlement were rooted. The second proprietor, Francis Shaw, also stands in this Boston context.

Francis Shaw (1721‑1784) was a descendant of John Shaw who, as early as 1646 had been a member of the Ancient and Honourable Artillery Company when John Winthrop was the founding governor of Boston. Generations of respectable people followed, culminating in Francis the Proprietor. He was the son of a tailor called Thomas Shaw who would die at the age of 80 in 1759 and would be buried at King's Chapel, the oldest Anglican church in New England. Francis Shaw was in his family of birth the third child and second son, occupying an inconspicuous place in tailor Thomas's family circle. Like his father, Francis lived and worked in the busy and crowded North End of Boston where, described as a tailor, he purchased his house in Fish Street where all of his children would be born. In his growing family, dense interconnections would develop not only between the children and the families with which they intermarried, but also between those in Boston and those in Gouldsboro. Robert Gould never lived on the eastern Maine coast, yet he was important enough to have given his name to the fledgling township even very early in its history. If Robert Gould's life was exclusively Bostonian, the Shaws began movements of residential permanency, in different degrees, from Fish Street to Township Number Three. The family became part of the permanency of the settlement and its development. It was a family in transition. A Boston family with Gouldsboro interests gradually became a Gouldsboro family with Boston connections.

Lydia Dickman, the first wife of Francis Shaw, senior, made this stitch work sampler in her youth-- a typical demonstration of the skills expected of a prospective Boston housewife. It reads "Lydia Dickman is my name and England is my nation and Boston is my dwelling place and Christ is my salvation- Done in my thirteenth year May 18 1735." [Sampler—Smithsonian National Museum of American History]

After several years' time Francis Shaw would move out from the circle of tailors into the mercantile world that was the essential basis of Boston's life and society in the eighteenth century. At the age of twenty four he married Lydia Dickman on the first of January 1745. The little story of Francis Shaw's first family is characteristic of much of the tragedy that befell the Shaw family, fairly common throughout the colonial world. Their child Thomas was born less than a year after their marriage, in December 1745. Lydia Dickman Shaw died the day after Christmas 1746, shortly before her second wedding anniversary and little more than two weeks after her baby's first birthday. That baby Thomas, named for his grandfather the old tailor of Boston, died 14 September 1747, three months short of two years old. The widowed father Francis, now left without wife or child, married a week after the baby's death a woman named Sarah Burt, daughter of fine and celebrated Boston silversmith Benjamin Burt. By this sturdy woman Francis Shaw's first child, Francis Shaw jr, appeared in the narrow streets of Boston and in the wider world on 28 July 1748. Three days later he was baptized in nearby Christ Church, Salem Street, now known also as Old North Church. All of the Shaw children would be baptized there, in the same congregation as the Gould family. Neighbors of the Shaws

42

in North Square were the Reveres whose son Paul would become Boston's most celebrated silversmith.

Through the nearly twenty years between 1748 and 1765, Sarah Burt Shaw bore eleven children. Oddly enough, the last – another Thomas like Francis's first born son by Lydia Dickman ‑ died at the age of seven months. Much later, during the occupation of Boston by the British in the Revolutionary War, British officers Major Pitcairn and Lieutenant Wragg would be billeted on the Shaw family. The house where they lived would be described in the tax list of 1798 as a wooden dwelling 486 feet square, three stories high, with eighteen windows. In that same house Wragg would disparage the Massachusetts rebels, and when the Shaw sons grew angry Major Pitcairn would arbitrate. Francis Shaw was called "a respectable tailor whose family was large."

In the Shaw family's neighborhood was the well-known house of Paul Revere, now a national monument. [Library of Congress photo]

Francis Shaw Senior, son of tailor Thomas and father of many children, was one of the triumvirate to whom the General Court of Massachusetts confirmed, in February 1762, the grant of Township Number Three on Frenchman's Bay in the eastern lands newly acquired from France by Great Britain. With him in that enterprise were Robert Gould, two years older than Shaw, and Nathan Jones, thirteen years younger. These men were now spreading out from Boston and, in line with the mercantile foundation of the town, were

43

casting their lot in with the developing country to the "east'ard." It would prove to be the undoing of Gould and of the Shaws. Clearly Robert Gould, who left no descendants to survive carrying his name, was important to Shaw whose family carried forward several generations of Shaw men bearing the name Robert Gould. The name was preserved as well in the township called Gouldsboro two hundred miles eastward of Boston.

The codicil to Shaw's will in 1784, written only days before his death, mentions silver plate (probably made, at least in part, by Benjamin Burt), and cash, bonds, mortgages and notes of hand: all expected in the estate of a businessman. Gouldsboro, however, the major investment the Shaws made, nearly took them down, as it did the great London trading house of Lane, Son and Fraser, to whom the Shaws, Gould and Nathan Jones were heavily mortgaged at the onset of the Revolutionary War which ruined them all. Mr. Francis Shaw senior, who had served as Collector of Taxes for the Town of Boston, died on Monday the 18th of October 1784, three years almost to the day after the surrender of General Cornwallis at Yorktown, Virginia. He was buried from Christ Church, Salem Street in nearby Copp's Hill Burying Ground. His children married well and successfully. Four of them are of special interest.

The most famous was Major Samuel Shaw (1754-1794). Himself a merchant in Boston, he was an officer in the Revolutionary War and aide-de-camp to General Henry Knox, another Bostonian and Proprietor of the Waldo Patent in Maine. Samuel lived some time at Gouldsboro. Probably through the influence of his old commander General Knox, he was appointed by President Washington as first American consul to Canton in China. He sailed in the *Empress* to Canton in 1784, the year of his father's death. Returning to America, he had built at Braintree a merchant ship of 820 tons, the largest then on the seas, and in her he sailed again to Canton where she was sold. On his return voyage he died at sea off the Cape of Good Hope at the age of thirty nine. His wife Hannah Phillips (1756-1833) was sister of William Phillips (1746-1827) who had been a member of the Boston Tea Party in the turmoil leading to the Revolution. Her sister Abigail (born 1745) married Josiah Quincy. Their son Josiah Quincy (1772-1864), Massachusetts politician on state and national levels, mayor of Boston, and president of Harvard College, wrote a memoir of Samuel Shaw, his uncle, following Shaw's death.

Three other sons of Francis Shaw the Proprietor were of more immediate relevance to Gouldsboro in its foundational years. Francis Shaw jr, first-born son of Sarah Burt, the Proprietor's indomitable second wife, was born in Boston in the family house in Fish Street in 1748. As a teenage boy

Francis jr was interested in growing up, interested in the ways of his father, when the triumvirate of Gould, Shaw and Jones received the grant of Number Three. As agent in Gouldsboro for his father and Robert Gould he was more involved than his father could be in the daily life of the settlement because he actually made his home there. He married Hannah Nickels, daughter of Captain William Nickels, another Bostonian settling in Maine, and she also had been born in Boston in 1754. Captain Nickels also was connected with Gouldsboro as agent for Lane, Son and Fraser. Of their six children, only two – William Nickels Shaw and Robert Gould Shaw – both

An 18th Century Boston merchant's house such as the Shaws might own. This has storage for goods and a residence upstairs.—[The Marshall-Hancock House, Marshall Street, Boston; Library of Congress photo]

born in Gouldsboro, would marry and produce children. Son William lived in Steuben until his death. Robert was thirteen when, having "ambitions beyond Gouldsboro," he was sent to Boston to live with Uncle Samuel and receive an education.

Francis Shaw Jr was an officer of the militia in eastern Maine, taking a leadership role during the Revolutionary War, and was especially involved in treating with the Indians. In 1775 he was made captain of the militia in Gouldsboro. In February 1777 he was in Boston with some of the St John Indians and the Council of Massachusetts Bay ordered him "to procure a small vessel and convey the St John Indians . . . to their home; and that [he] proceed with the letter from Gen. Washington, which he has in his care, to the Indian Country, and there deliver and remain among said Indians at least six weeks . . . and to use his best exertions to confirm said Indians in the interest of this Continent." For this work his pay as fifteen pounds sterling a month, and his rank was raised to major.

A modern view of Copp's Hill Burying Ground in Boston, last resting-place of Gouldsboro proprietor Francis Shaw, senior.

He was a founding member and first senior warden of the Masonic lodge in Machias in 1779 and, like his father before him, was a supporting member of the Episcopal Charitable Society of Boston. He died only six months after his father, at the age of thirty seven, and was buried, not in Boston, but in Steuben graveyard. It was early spring, when perhaps the peepers were beginning in Gouldsboro, and he was insolvent and heavily in debt, attended during his last illness by Dr Benjamin Alline, who also had settled in the town. Commissioners were appointed by the court to sort out the various financial tangles of his estate. In their daunting task food and rum were provided them. Several mills that were the economic basis of this lumbering settlement were involved in the transactions: Tunk Mill, upper Western Mill, the Lower Mill, Whitten's Mill and – most colorful of all, Four Bachelors Mill, where Samuel Joy, millwright who had moved to Gouldsboro from the Kennebec River, charged the estate six shillings for "one days work on the mill Four Bachelors." Francis's widow Hannah married Jacob Townsley, widower of her sister Margaret, and lived on in Steuben until 1835.

William Shaw, Francis senior's younger son, was born in Boston in 1756 and "lived in Gouldsboro many years." Like his brother Francis Jr he was a member of the Machias Masonic lodge. In 1785 he was appointed Justice of the Peace for Gouldsboro in Lincoln County where Gouldsboro then lay. In about 1799 William Shaw and Judith his wife moved to Quincy, Massachusetts where he bought a farm if eighty acres. His residence in Gouldsboro was ended. His death came suddenly. "Died August 13, 1803, William Shaw, aged 47, at Charlemont, on his return from a journey to the Springs," where he had apparently gone for his health. After his departure from

46

Gouldsboro he sold several pieces of land there that he still owned. In November 1803 his widow Judith and nephew Robert Gould Shaw "were empowered by the Supreme Judicial Court at Boston . . . to sell . . .said intestate's real estate to the amount of $7700 for the payment of his debts." Seven tracts that he still owned in Gouldsboro were sold. Other lots were sold as well in an effort to meet his debts. Financial ruin still involved the proprietors and their families.

The son of Francis Shaw senior who had the most lasting impact on the life of Gouldsboro was John Shaw, born in Boston in 1750. He was two years younger than Francis Jr and several years older than Samuel and William. He was a resident of Gouldsboro for most of his short life. His years were few, with little opportunity to be active in the town. His marriage to Sarah Jones, daughter of Nathan Jones, united the families of the two proprietors, and made a Gouldsboro family. A son, Nathan Shaw, namesake of his grandfather, was born in the town in January 1780. Sometime that same year, with an only child less than a year old, John Shaw died. His widow Sarah married an English sea captain, William Robert Emmanuel Boyd of Portland, and by him had several children, all connected to the town of Gouldsboro though born in Weston, Massachusetts.. Nathan Shaw

---

THE SONS AND GRANDSONS of FRANCIS SHAW SENIOR in GOULDSBORO

Francis Shaw Sr. (1721-1784)   *In Boston*
m. (1) Lydia Dickson, (2) Sarah Burt

HIS SONS IN GOULDSBORO

* **Francis (junior 1748-1785)**   *in Gouldsboro from late 1760s?*
    m. Hannah Nickles (Capt. Wm. Nickles' daughter)
    =<u>Robert Gould</u> (1776 -1853) m. Elizabeth Willard
                    -*born in Gouldsboro; many descendants*
    = William Nickles (1783- 1845) m. Nancy Stevens - *born Gouldsboro- lived in Steuben*
    = George (1778-1789)   - *born in Gouldsboro, died at Grand Manan*

John (1750-1780)   *in Gouldsboro from 1770s, died there*
    m. Sarah Jones (Nathan Jones' daughter)
    =John jr (1778-1800)   *died at sea*
    = <u>Nathan (1780-1867)</u> m. 1810 Eunice Bradish Smith (a Cobb descendant)

*Samuel (1754 -1794)   *in Gouldsboro ca. 1770s - early 1780s*
    m. Hannah Phillips - Boston)

*William (1756 - 1803)   *in Gouldsboro ca. 1780s-90s*
    m. Judith

47

became involved in the affairs of Gouldsboro until his death there in 1867. His offices in the town included town clerk, selectman, and representative. His wife Eunice Bradish Smith (1791-1859), was granddaughter of General David Cobb. Colonel John Black officiated at their marriage in Gouldsboro in 1810. The nine children of Nathan and Eunice Shaw married and raised families in eastern Maine. The family was no longer of Boston. They were of Gouldsboro.

Sources

*Maine: Hancock County Deeds, Lincoln County Deeds and Probate
*Massachusetts: Suffolk County Deeds and Probate
*Esther Forbes, *Paul Revere and the World He Lived In*
*Mary Kent Davey Babcock, *Christ Church, Salem Street, Boston*
*Frederick Kidder, *Military Operations in Maine and Nova Scotia in the War of the Revolution.*
*Boston Tax List, 1798
Maine Historical Magazine
*Grace Wood Clark, *Historical Researches of Gouldsboro, Maine*

As a militia officer in the Revolution, Francis Shaw Jr. worked to protect the Patriot base at the port of Machias—as it appeared here in the 1770s. He was enlisted in 1777 to deal with Passamaquoddy and Maliseet Indians to help defend against British attacks. [From the Des Barres "Atlantic Neptune" chart—Library of Congress]

Chapter 4

GOULDSBORO IN THE REVOLUTIONARY WAR

The famous 1775 "minute men" of Lexington, Massachusetts, are memorialized in this statue of a humble farmer militiaman much like those in early Gouldsboro, called out in homespun clothes to stand in defense of the community. If outfitted for a campaign a Gouldsboro militiaman would add only a hat and coat, canteen, and perhaps a blanket. [GFDL image]

In this talk given in August of 2005, Rev. Joy presents the heartfelt testimony of early Gouldsboro's Revolutionary soldiers, placing them in the broad context of the struggle for survival on the downeast coast during the desperate times of the 1770s and 80s.

℘

By the time of the Revolutionary War, Gouldsboro was still only little more than ten years old, in essence a frontier mill town whose prime product was wood and lumber: pine boards for building; spars, booms, masts, bowsprits and keels for building vessels of rock maple and oak. All of eastern Maine was still a newly minted part of the British Empire, filled with settlers who were economically desperate, marginalized in life and disaffected with the existing social order from which they had fled. The settlement—though legally termed a plantation, a township, or sometimes a "town," was unorganized, not incorporated as a legal township, but entirely dependent on support from the proprietors in Boston. It was out of the main stream and dependent in many ways.

Gouldsboro was on the ragged edge of the American world and of military action during the war of revolution. The events of the war in eastern Maine were for the two-fold purpose of basic self-preservation on one hand, and of holding the east for Massachusetts on the other. People uprooted from earlier homes in various places, disturbed by financial crises and disasters, were alienated from traditional society with their backs against the wall. They were ready to fight for what little they had, like hungry dogs at war for a scrap.

In 1775, after a decade or more of unrest and confrontation between the colonies and the British Parliament, the show-down was approaching. Issues of taxes and representation, subtler issues of great distance, poor communication, gradual cultural change and alienation during the century and a half since the colonies' beginning, brought the approaching climax. In March 1770 came the Boston Massacre when civilians were shot by edgy British troops. In December 1773 the Boston Tea Party made a bold and somewhat violent statement against taxes on imported goods. Unrest and dissatisfaction, taking an open and active turn issuing in violence in and near Boston, resulted in more British troops brought in to quiet the unrest. Then in April 1775, at the villages of Lexington and

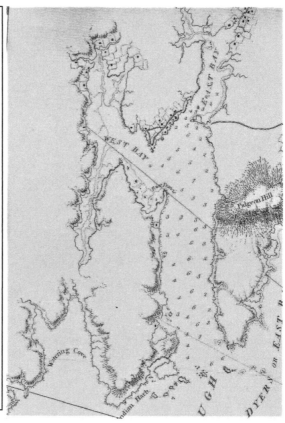

The sparse population of early eastern Gouldsboro settlements is shown in this British Admiralty map of 1772, with homesteads -- shown as black dots -- only in the upper reaches of Gouldsboro Bay. Houses appear at the right at "East Bay" in Town Number 4, (Steuben); ands on the point in the center (Gouldsboro Point), and on the left at "West Bay." But southern areas are basically unoccupied. Prospect Bay is shown only as a water supply for Admiralty ships. (nb.- "Pidgeon Hill" later became Eagle Hill.) [The "Atlantic Neptune," 1775; U.S. Library of Congress.]

Concord,   occurred armed confrontation and blood shedding on a larger scale. "By the rude bridge that arched the flood. . . the embattled farmers stood and fired the shot heard round the world." Push had now come to shove. The time for parleying and negotiation was nearly, if not completely, past.

The shots fired in Lexington and Concord reverberated in down east Maine. In August 1775, Gouldsboro, Narraguagus, Number Four and Pleasant River petitioned the General Court of Massachusetts "relative to the distress'd Situation of those Towns." In response the Court authorized a company of fifty men, including officers, to be raised and stationed in those towns, "with 100 weight of powder, 500 flints and ball equivalent," to be sent by sea from Boston to Falmouth, then on down east to Captain Alexander Campbell. War had begun in earnest.

It is very hard for us now to realize that Britain with the might of its empire was the deadly enemy, while yet the people of Gouldsboro, by blood and by heritage, saw themselves as British to a person. Since that revolutionary era the whirligig of time has turned the world upside down, even as the British played the tune of that name in Yorktown, Virginia, at their final defeat. Today the British embassy in Washington, with its diplomatic license plate number 1, is testimony to our long and close alliance and affection with the United Kingdom It is very hard to realize now the venom of the animosity against British government in 1775.

Captain Daniel Sullivan, who led the largest Gouldsboro militia unit early in the Revolution, was captured in 1782 by the British and imprisoned. He died in the dungeon hulk HMS Jersey, [Engraving of 1851-Library of Congress]

The military organization in Gouldsboro and all of down east Maine was created in militia groups, composed of men who served in various capacities and times as soldiers. It was not a standing army like the Continental line that fought in Boston, New York and New Jersey. It was a kind of ad hoc army. Militias were composed of ordinary citizens who enlisted for set periods of several months. They met regularly at militia musters for instruction, discipline and drill and were not called into active service except for specific situations. It was a matter of constant availability but not of constant service. They "continued equipped & in readiness at a minute's warning," said John Gubtail, an old soldier, and so they were called "minutemen," leaving to fight at a moment's notice.

Twenty two militia groups under various commanding officers can be identified as having at least one man from Gouldsboro. Of those, the most frequently called into service were the companies serving under the brothers Captains Henry and Reuben Dyer of Number Four (now Steuben), Captain Stephen Smith of Machias, and Captain

Daniel Sullivan of Frenchman's Bay (now Sullivan). Most of these companies were component parts of the Sixth Lincoln County Regiment under Colonel Benjamin Foster of Machias.

The militia companies involving the largest numbers of Gouldsboro men were those of Captain Daniel Sullivan, twenty two men; Captains Reuben Dyer and Samuel Libby, nineteen men each; Captain Henry Dyer, seventeen men; Captain Francis Shaw, thirteen men; and Captain Eleazer Crabtree, eight men. Though Daniel Sullivan had the largest single number of soldiers from Gouldsboro, the Dyer brothers together had the largest total, thirty six.

The soldiers were all settlers struggling to wrest a living in a hard place. One of the privates was Richard Fassett. He owned 100 acres on West Bay that had belonged to his father in law John Walker. Born in Great Britain in 1748, Fassett at fourteen had been a cabin boy in the flagship of Admiral Saunders and his supporter in the great battle of Quebec on the Plains of Abraham in 1762. That having been said, the war was not romantic, though at this distance it may seem so.

David McCullough describes the nature of the militiamen. "Few of the men had what would pass as a uniform. Field officers were all but indistinguishable from the troops they led. Not only were most men unwashed and often unshaven, they were clad in a bewildering variety of this and that, largely whatever they, or others at home, had been able to throw together before they trudged off to war . . . they wore heavy homespun coats and shirts, these often in tatters from constant wear, britches of every color and condition, cowhide shoes and

The Americans' attempt to retake Castine in 1779 was foiled by hesitant naval action, allowing the British fleet to sweep in to destroy them. The British fleet is shown pursuing the Americans, as depicted in an 1814 London engraving of a painting by John Thomas Serres. [MHS collection]

moccasins, and, on their heads, old broad-brimmed felt hats, farmers' straw hats or striped bandanas tied sailor-fashion. . . . It was an army of men accustomed to hard work, hard work being the common lot. They were familiar with adversity and making do in a harsh climate. Resourceful, handy with tools, they could drive a yoke of oxen or "hove up" a stump or tie a proper knot as readily as butcher a hog or mend a pair of shoes. They knew from experience, most of them, the hardships and setbacks of life. Preparing for the worse was second nature. Rare was the man who had never seen someone die."

Military action in eastern Maine extended from Machias on the east to Majorbagaduce, (today Castine) on the west, the two largest centers of population. Gouldsboro is midway between them. It became vital for the patriots to hold Machias, the easternmost anchor of the population in eastern Maine, and it was crucial that all the small coastal settlements stand together. The first naval battle of the war occurred in June 1775 around the vessel *Margaretta*, a small warship in the royal navy. Ichabod Jones of Machias had made an agreement with the British then occupying Boston that he would send wood, vital for fuel, by his ships to occupied Boston. In turn they would allow him to pass the Boston harbor blockade loaded with goods to sell in Machias. His ships were being guarded by *Margaretta*. She was attacked and captured by the local Americans. Most of the later action involving the defense of Machias took place in 1777 when soldiers from Gouldsboro, forty six miles away, had to walk on what was "merely a path cut through the words without any attention to the ground and terribly bad."

Majorbagaduce, now Castine, at the mouth of Penobscot River, was occupied by 700 British troops from Halifax, Nova Scotia. The two-fold purpose was to protect British shipping in the east from American privateers, and to form a nucleus of a new colony to be called New Ireland for loyalist refugees from New England. A flotilla of forty vessels was launched in June 1779 from Boston, now freed from British occupation, in the "Penobscot Expedition," and was joined in part by the militia from Gouldsboro and the rest of eastern Maine. The goal was to drive the British from Majorbagaduce. It was a total failure.

There was also constant threat to settlements fronting on the coast requiring constant vigilance and often action. "British cruisers frequently came off the coast," an elderly man remembered in 1832, "& often for the purposes of plunder entered the Bays & creeks in the neighborhood of Gouldsboro & as often did this Declarent & his compeers let them know the country would not be surrendered. He can truly say that his services in this way were for the last five years of the war equally of service . . . and all performed without compensation except the satisfaction of having served his country."

An unnamed British ship, "a British privateer," chased an American vessel from Jones's Cove. Satisfaction was provided to the Americans when "on going out the Privateer got aground." John Gubtail "was very desirous of boarding said vessel but it was thought too dangerous." The British ship *Viper*, idling in the sea outside Gouldsboro harbor for six days in August 1776, hindered Francis Shaw

Downeast Mainers were harassed by patrolling British vessels of this type— a typical British "sloop of war" of the Revolution era. [Painting by Charles Brooking - National Maritime Museum, Greenwich, London]

and some of his men from sailing eastward to Machias. Shaw called the vessel "the greatest Scourge . . . since the commencement of the present War." In March 1779 the British schooner *Liverpool* from Nova Scotia plundered Shaw's store on Gouldsboro Point "to the Amount of Three Thousand Pounds," a very hefty amount of money.

In addition, the lumber trade which was the lifeblood of infant Gouldsboro – then barely ten years old – was interrupted by the constantly cruising British threat. A desperate appeal to the government of Massachusetts in spring 1778 detailed the problems facing the settlement. "The Inhabitants of the Township of Gouldsborough are in a Deplorable Situation occasioned by the total Stagnation of the Lumber Trade, upon which we mostly Depended for a Living, and the Frequent Allarms, whereby we was obliged to March to Machias the last year, Intirely prevented us from Raising any Provisions for our Familys, or procuring Hay for our Cattle which has occasion'd the Loss of many of them during the Winter & Spring, and now leaves [us] hardly able to do [our] Spring work on [our] Farms." Later that summer Francis Shaw reported "in behalf of the Inhabitants of the Township of Gouldsborough" that "many of them [are] Intirely destitute of Bread for a month past." In response the Council of Massachusetts Bay "Ordered That the Board of War be . . . directed to deliver to Francis Shaw Esqr . . . One Hundred bushels Indian Corn for the use of the distressed Inhabitants of the Township of Goldsboro in the County of Lincoln."

Peace was reached at last at Yorktown in 1781 with the final surrender under General Cornwallis, and Gouldsboro moved forward. There remains, however, one voice – small, obscure and unhistoric, very different from most of the veterans but an unusual part of the story connected to Gouldsboro that deserves to be heard. The voice is thin and fragile but intense and vivid.

Alexander McCaleb [or McKillip] left numerous progeny and bloodlines scattered throughout Gouldsboro and beyond. His voice is one faint and final echo of the Revolutionary struggle that speaks in a peculiarly human and winsomely living way. He was born in 1761 to a family obviously of Scottish origin who had settled in Albany County, New York. When he was fifteen, in the spring of 1776, he enlisted as a drummer boy "under Captain Mott of Colonel Macdougalls regiment New York troops." As a man of eighty two living in Steuben, his story is told in his own words.

"I . . . marched to Fort Edward then to Lake George thence to Saint Johns, Chamblee and Montreal in Canada & came to Quebec by sledge on the ice from whence we were driven by superior force (Burgoines army) and retreated back to Stillwater. I then enlisted for three years or during the war in Captain Coops Company of Colonel Goose van Schaik's 14 New York regiment, commonly called . . . and during the last term of service we marched through the Jerseys and took up quarters at Valley Forge and was at the Battle of Monmouth and the taking of Burgoyne . . . . In the fall of the year 1780 at a place above Albany called New City (now Troy) myself and five others were surprised and taken by the British and carried to ticonderoga from thence carried to St Johns in Canada where I remained one year and a half or more. From thence I made my escape on board of a British schooner in disguise, masters name was Merritt, Schooners name was Gaspy, in which schooner I proceeded to Halifax from thence by land to a place called Copycutt from thence went on board a vessel bound to Passimiquada now Eastport from thence by land to this town, in which town and the adjoining town of Gouldsborough I have resided ever since."

He observes that "as death has been continually thinning our ranks from the day of our Independence to the present moment, there is now but a small remnant remaining. . . . I know of no one living with whom I associated in those times that tried mens souls – after I made my escape from the British in Canada and came to this place I took up my abode here where I have remained ever since . . . the long lapse of time and the remote distance I am placed from any of my comrades is clear.. . ."

This re-enactor group shows a typical unit of local militia of the 1760s and 70s, raised like the Gouldsboro men to serve under a local captain such as Daniel Sullivan or Francis Shaw. [Fort Dobbs militia re-enactment.]

Several testimonials amplify the picture of the old soldier. Nathan Shaw of West Gouldsboro, aged sixty two, testified that "some time between the years 1792 & 94 Alexander McCaleb came into said town of Gouldsboro where he soon after married Hannah Young daughter of Noah Young and . . . lived in said town for at least twenty years . . . ." (Parenthetically, Alexander McCaleb's father in law Noah Young, a native of Dover, New Hampshire and settler in Gouldsboro in 1766, had himself served as Private in the Gouldsboro militia when he was fifty years old). "I was well acquainted with him," Shaw went on to say, "[I] have frequently heard him relate his services in the Revolutionary War, and that he was in the Battle of Monmouth under Genl Washington. . . ."

Nicholas Thomas, an upstanding citizen of Hancock County, had known Alexander McCaleb for fifty years, since his father had hired McCaleb, a tailor, to make him a coat. "In September 1803 at a General Muster of the Militia at Ellsworth, while I was in a tent," Thomas recalled, "near the aforesaid ground in company with Elkanah Remick, a revolutionary soldier. . . Alexander McKillip came into the tent. He soon recalected [sic] said Elkanah Remick and made himself known to him who greatly recalected McKillip. They shook hands together, bought some rum or other Spiritous Liquer [sic] and after drinking it they both began to relate their adventures in the army at the South. McKillip took up a drum and beat several marches, Ramack observed to him that he had heard him play the same tune while he was with him in the army or while he was in the service as a soldier." There yet remains one small but living picture.

The little incident of a surprise reunion of old companions McCaleb and Remick on the bright early fall day in September 1803 was amplified by Samuel Moore of Steuben. ". . . . drumming was a favorite amusement in his old age and was usually present at Military training to Drum for the Company."

We are perhaps struck by some profound contrasts present in this old soldier's little story. We have General Washington, plantation master in Virginia and first president of the United States, and Alexander McCaleb, a simple tailor of Steuben and Gouldsboro who signed with the mark of the unlettered. We have Valley Forge, and Yorktown; Machias, and Majorbagaduce; British general Burgoyne, and Dutch New York American officers ; a stately white plantation house called Mount Vernon on the Potomac River near Washington, D.C.,s and a simple brown tombstone in a small overgrown graveyard on Pigeon Hill in Steuben where Alexander McCaleb has his obscure last resting place. All of these mark the contrasts between the Revolution in distant places and in Gouldsboro in eastern Maine. Each was important, and each has a living place in the history of that complex reality that is called America. That contrast and variety is essential to a faithful telling of the tale. Honor is not reckoned by size but by fidelity.

The sound of a drum beating marches for a long dead and disbanded army far from the time and the places of their conflict celebrates their heroism and as well the memory of a time that was already far distant and long ago.

Sources

*James S. Leamon, *Revolution Downeast: The War for American Independence in Maine.*
*John Howard Ahlin, *Maine Rubicon: Downeast Settlers during the American Revolution.*
*George E. Buker, *The Penobscot Expedition*
Documentary History of Maine
Massachusetts Soldiers and Sailors of the Revolutionary War
*David McCulloch, *1776*
*Revolutionary War pensions, National Archives

Chapter 5

THE NEW PROPRIETOR :
WILLIAM BINGHAM

William Bingham started building his fortune during the Revolution as a commercial and diplomatic agent for the Continental Congress, dealing with the French in the West Indies. Following the war he went on to serve in the Pennsylvania legislature and the U.S. Senate until he retired to England to manage and develop his extensive holdings in real estate. [Library of Congress image]

The Reverend Joy gave this talk in August of 2004, outlining the career of this influential man of the world. William Bingham saw very little of Gouldsboro, but his actions to regulate the town's land ownership were to have lasting effects on local properties well into the present day.

§

The first proprietors of Gouldsboro -- Nathan Jones, Robert Gould and Francis Shaw – were based in Boston, from which the settlement and development of the town were managed in the beginning. By the end of the century, following the cataclysm of the Revolutionary War, one new proprietor appeared. His name was William Bingham. His base was not Boston but Philadelphia. His great purchase of land changed the history of Maine and the history of Gouldsboro. It connected this peninsula to a new and even broader world than that of the first proprietors, a farther reach and a wider sophistication. Bingham was a man at home in the courts of Europe. He was an intimate friend of the founders of our government: Washington, Jefferson, Hamilton and the rest. The Revolutionary War that took a nearly fatal toll on the Gouldsboro settlement in economic disaster provided a wider stage for Bingham in his service to the fledgling Republic. An important part of understanding the history of Gouldsboro is to see Bingham in the same frame as the woodlands and overgrown fields, country roads and villages, seaside and abandoned farmsteads of the Gouldsboro peninsula. An extreme contrast nonetheless represents an important connection. Although he had very little immediate contact with the town, he played a huge and vital role in its life through the three quarters of the peninsula that he bought and in which, through his agents, he took great interest.

William Bingham was born in 1752 in Philadelphia, the most populous city in the British colonies of North America. His father began as a saddler but evolved into mercantile pursuits especially in terms of the rum trade with the West Indies. The first settler of the name, a goldsmith in London, emigrated to New Jersey in the 1680s. His son located in Philadelphia as a blacksmith. Bingham's mother, Molly Stamper, was the daughter of a mayor of Philadelphia. The Bingham family, of some means, was – like the original proprietors of Gouldsboro -- English, Anglican and established.

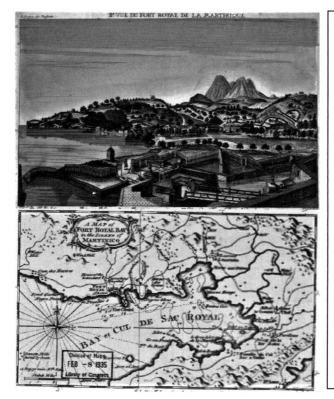

The Caribbean port of Fort Royal in French Martinique was a prime location for American efforts during the Revolution to woo French support, while Bingham"s own privateers raided British shipping. He grew rich while serving as Continental agent to the French here and in St Pierre. [Print by Francois Denis; map from Library of Congress]

Following the early death of his father, Bingham was placed in a Quaker counting house where, learning mercantile pursuits, he discovered a natural aptitude for business and ability with money. As a very young man he was named secretary of the Committee of Secret Correspondence in Philadelphia. His particular effort was to involve France on the side of the British American colonies in their revolt against the Crown and Parliament. He served for three years in Martinique, a French Caribbean colony, where he grew wealthy as a tradesman and owner of privateers.

At the end of the Revolutionary War, in 1782 William Bingham with two other merchants founded the mercantile firm of Bingham, Inglis and Gilmor. Part of their work was to buy significant tracts of land in Pennsylvania and New York to develop industry and commerce. These purchases included more than 26,000 acres that includes the present-day city of Binghamton, New York. Always a public-spirited man aiming at the total development of the community, he was one of the founders of Carlisle College, one of the founding members of the

Bank of North America, and a supporter of the Lancaster Turnpike in Pennsylvania.

With the return of peace between the newly free United States and the mother country Great Britain, Bingham, with a sense of business and money to be made, went to live in London. His wife Anne Willing, daughter of a Philadelphia judge, whom he married in Christ Church, Philadelphia, in 1780, and his daughter Ann, a toddler born in January 1782, accompanied him. They took a house in Harley Street, Cavendish Square, where the second daughter Maria was born in December 1783. Among his new friends was the Earl of Shelburne, Marquis of Lansdowne, who had been consistently friendly to American independence and interests. Entertained by the Earl of Shelburne at his country house, Bowood Park, in Wiltshire, Bingham through many new connections pursued prospects of trade between Britain and America. The Binghams also spent much time at the spas in Bath, pictured clearly in some of the contemporary writing of Jane Austen. Among new acquaintances met in the circle of Lord Shelburne was Francis Baring, merchant banker, director of the East India Company, and liberal Whig member of Parliament.

During the years when the Binghams lived in Europe, they travelled widely on the continent. In Holland they saw John Adams, later President, and in Paris Benjamin Franklin and Thomas Jefferson. Jefferson was not fond of William Bingham but very friendly with his wife Anne. At Versailles, as guest of John Adams, Bingham was presented to King Louis XVI, later beheaded with Marie Antoinette his queen in the Reign of Terror of the French Revolution. Abigail Adams said that Bingham "came flourishing out to be presented to his most Christian Majesty, the King of France, with his four horses and three servants, in all the pomp of an American merchant." In 1786, Bingham was presented to the Court of George III in London.

Later in 1786 the Binghams returned home to Philadelphia. In that city, at the Constitutional Convention in May 1787, George Washington's diary notes: "Dined and drank tea at Mr. Bingham's, splendor shown" – this from the master of Mount Vernon plantation. As a financial expert, William Bingham served as advisor to Alexander Hamilton on tax and treasury laws in setting up the monetary system of the United States. In April 1790 he was one of the pallbearers for Benjamin Franklin in the churchyard of Christ Church while the bells tolled a muffled peal. In tribute to the man whose body he helped bear to its grave, Bingham commissioned a statue of Franklin for the

Library Company of Philadelphia. In the same year he served as Speaker of the House of Representatives of Pennsylvania.

It was a tenuous time for the new country. In the early 1790s inflation created a financial panic. Those with liquid assets were able to make great addition to massive real estate purchases in northwest Pennsylvania, Bingham was approached by a friend who had bought certain lands in the District of Maine for which he was now unable to pay. Bingham agreed to take over his interest in those lands. Thus William Bingham pledged himself to purchase some two million acres and optioned for another million. It amounted to about one ninth of the entire area of Maine.

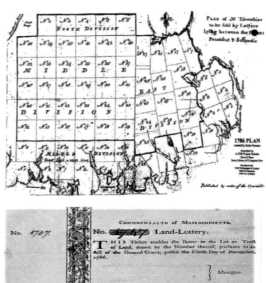

Massachusetts unsuccessfully tried in 1786-87 to raise funds by selling lottery plots of its land in Eastern Maine-- territory which later in the 1790s was bought by Bingham.

Lottery plot tickets like this raised very little money for just a few lots, leaving the bulk of the land to investors like General Knox, and eventually to Bingham. [Library of Congress]

General Henry Knox (1750-1806) was George Washington's friend and favorite general. He was ample in ambition as he was ample in appetite and girth, and in the end he choked to death on a chicken bone. He was a man, as he was described, "of expensive tastes but moderate resources," having risen from a bookstore owner in Boston through a fortunate marriage to become a Maine landlord. Colonel William Duer (1747-1799) was an Englishman who settled in New York in 1768. Active in the military and in politics, he was imprisoned for debt in the financially turbulent 1790s. In July 1791 these two men, Knox and Duer, bought two tracts of land in the District of Maine from the government of Massachusetts which was trying at the time to raise money to cancel governmental debts incurred by the recent war. Included in that purchase were a little over two million acres sold at a cost of ten cents per acre. In the spring of 1792 the investors spoke for another million acres at a cost of twenty and twenty one cents per acre, including the eastern half of Mount Desert Island. They contracted with Massachusetts by a down payment of $10,000 and the promise to pay $400,00 to $500,000 remaining. Duer's wealth collapsed in the shaky financial weather of that final decade of the century. Knox was left alone with staggering debt. He badly needed a partner with resources. Enter William Bingham, friend, fellow Federalist and financial resource extraordinaire. In January 1793 the transfer was made. With the rest of the land, he had bought 8000 acres of former Shaw land in Gouldsboro at twenty-five cents and acre. That purchase gave Bingham a coastal township that could be developed as an ocean outlet for his extensive inland holdings.

Even Bingham, however, found himself overtaxed and over extended. Wealthy as he was, Bingham needed more money for development. America was just getting started and money was not flourishing even for the wealthy. Bingham wrote to General Knox: "Viewing the distressed situation in which I am placed for want of funds, I am persuaded of the propriety of again attempting the European market." But in addition to new investors, he was also feeling the need to peddle some of the newly purchased lands in small

Revolutionary General Henry Knox inherited by marriage huge tracts of Mid-coast Maine, and attempted in 1791 to acquire the Massachusetts lottery plots in Eastern Maine. When he became overextended, William Bingham's investment in those lands and rescued Knox from bankruptcy, allowing him to retain his mansion in Thomaston, Maine. The mansion was later reconstructed as a museum. [Knox Museum]

parcels to individuals and American investor groups, for which, in the midst of his busy life some distance away in Philadelphia, he needed an on-the-spot agent in eastern Maine.

His selection fell upon another Revolutionary War general, David Cobb (1748-1830) of Taunton, Massachusetts. Cobb would become representative of the absentee proprietor for twenty five years and would become deeply engaged, on behalf first of the owner and then of his estate trustees, with the management of the Gouldsboro lands.

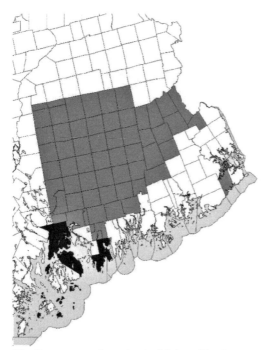

Bingham's vast inland holdings in Eastern Maine are shown here in light gray.

His coastal purchases of 1792, including eastern Mount Desert and Gouldsboro, are shown in dark gray. These gave him a much needed outlet to the sea for his inland timber lots. [Map by Thomas Mayer.]

In his search for a European investor, Bingham recalled Francis Baring, merchant banker of London, whom he had met through Lord Shelburne, and contacted him. Baring was interested in pursuing this potentially fertile source of investment and income in the fledgling United States. He determined to send his son Alexander (1774-1848), then aged twenty four, as his agent and representative. The young man arrived in Boston from England at the end of November 1795 where he met up with Cobb and Knox. He and Bingham first met on 16 January 1796. It was a momentous meeting.

That following summer a group which included, of course, William Bingham and Alexander Baring, but also Bingham's two daughters, came to Maine to scope out the land so recently bought. More was developing than just the huge tracts in Maine. In August 1798 Alexander Baring and Ann Bingham were married in Christ Church, Philadelphia. Thus it was that, in the words of Bingham's biographer, "the commercial alliance between Bingham and the Barings became a family connection." Bingham reflected, with a fair degree of understatement, that he viewed the union "with cheerful composure."

Bingham's glamorous wife, Anne Willing, was a Philadelphia beauty who was the subject of numerous paintings, including this one by Gilbert Stuart. [Philadelphia Museum of Art-Google Art Project]

By century's end, William Bingham had been a senator of the United States since 1795. He was considered the richest man and the largest landholder in the United States. A red letter day for him was 25 May 1799. On that date he sent the sum of $32,800 to Massachusetts as the final payment to that government for the millions of acres in Maine that he now owned in fee simple.

Anne Willing Bingham, considered one of the most beautiful women in America and sometime the delight of Thomas Jefferson in Paris died in Bermuda 11 May 1801, aged thirty seven, en route to Madeira. She was buried there in St George's Churchyard. Only very few weeks later, her widower William Bingham sailed with his daughters Nan and Maria to England. An infant son was left with his grandfather Judge Thomas Willing in Philadelphia. Now in England again, and the family connection with the Barings sealed, William Bingham spent much time in London and Bath. During this period he saw many old friends from his residence there twenty years before. A second marriage brought his family once more into intimate connection with the Barings. Maria Bingham had been married first, in Philadelphia in 1799, to the Comte de Tilly from whom she had been divorced. He would commit suicide in Brussels in 1816. Now, in 1802 she married, quietly in London, Henry Baring brother of her sister Ann's husband Alexander. By this second marriage, Mrs. Maria Baring gave birth to three sons and two daughters. She was divorced by her husband in 1824 and she married, third, the Marquis de Blaize in France. This second Baring marriage was announced to General Cobb in Gouldsboro by a letter from William Bingham in which he said "the interest you have always kindly taken in what regards my family induces me to mention the circumstance to you."

Of Ann Bingham Baring, an acquaintance wrote: "She had the reputation of heartlessness . . . she was very ambition of high social position [but] she received me with politeness and even kindness." Her sister Maria, veteran of two divorces, had married a wastrel as her third husband, who gambled compulsively and "used up money as fast as Maria could supply it." But the same acquaintance, who had commented on Mrs. Baring, said of Maria, "then an old woman but quite an amusing one. She had seen the world in many phases, and had plenty of anecdotes which she told pleasantly. She was a very amiable kind hearted woman." The Binghams had become largely a European family.

The Baring and Bingham money financed the Louisiana Purchase for the United States in 1802 in the presidency of Thomas Jefferson. Almost nine million dollars was the price advanced to the French government against the sale. The profit of Bingham and Baring from that loan was estimated at three million dollars.

William Bingham's health failed gradually. In Bath he signed his will on 30 January 1804, "being of sound and disposing mind and memory but low in health." By his will he appointed five trustees and empowered them to elect successors within six months of each vacancy. These original trustees represent the great breadth of his life and connections. "Alexander and Henry Baring of the City of London and Kingdom of Great Britain, Merchants, Robert Gilmore of the City of Baltimore, State of Maryland, Thomas Mayne Willing of the City of Philadelphia and State of Pennsylvania, Merchant, and Charles Willing Hare, of the same City and State, Esq. Devisees of all the Real Estate of William Bingham. . . ." Covered under the terms of the trust were all the unsold lands in Gouldsboro as well as throughout the Bingham Purchase in Maine.

Death came on 6 February, in his fifty second year. His funeral in Bath Abbey was followed by his interment there, near the back of the south aisle, beneath a monument that notes that he was "a native and Senator of the United States of America." In Philadelphia, Dr Benjamin Rush recollected William Bingham, the "new Proprietor of Gouldsboro in Maine." "He left an estate valued at three million of dollars, half a million of which was in stock of different kinds. He was pleasant in his manners, amiable in his temper, liberal but said not [to] be charitable. . . He acquired his immense estate by his own ingenuity . . . .In all his money speculations he was fortunate." The Trustees of William Bingham, operating under the terms and conditions of his English will, lasted until its final liquidation by the courts of the Common-wealth of Pennsylvania in November 1964.

In Gouldsboro, of which he was once three quarters owner, he has no memorial   *Sic transit gloria mundi.*

Sources

*Robert C. Alberts, *The Golden Voyage: The Life and Times of William Bingham 1752-1804.*
William Bingham's Maine Lands 1790-1820. Frederick S. Allis Jr, (ed.) in Publications of the Colonial Society of Massachusetts, Vol. XXXVI and XXXVII.
*Hancock County Deeds.

Chapter 6

"AS OTHERS SEE US" LORD BARING COMES TO GOULDSBORO

Alexander Baring is here portrayed after his elevation to the peerage, at about the time he was appointed to settle the "Aroostook War" border dispute with Canada. (Author's collection)

This talk, given by Rev. Joy in August of 2016, shows how early Gouldsboro was influenced by the great financial forces of the outside world. It also provides a perspective overview of the young town's settlement process.

℘

"O wad some pow'r the Giftie gie us
To see oursels as others see us."
Robert Burns, "To a Louse."

Gouldsboro was all about money. The original Puritan settlements in Massachusetts at Plymouth and Salem were theological enterprises, clearly enunciated by Governor John Winthrop and Governor William Bradford. They were founded and based in high Biblical vision. Governor Winthrop's "city on a hill" was to become a new England remade in a completed Reformation, a lamp on a lampstand to the nations of Europe. Early settlements were made in that light and with that definition. By the middle of the eighteenth century, however, that theological emphasis had been largely replaced by economic considerations. Following the defeat of France in the Seven Years War, Massachusetts secured the former French territory stretching from the east bank of Penobscot River to Passamaquoddy Bay. Very quickly it was surveyed in a sort of checkerboard pattern of potential townships and settlers began arriving almost willy-nilly. These were predominately individuals desperately down on their luck, burdened with debt, poor and needy, looking for some new place to begin a new life. There was no theology behind the process of settlement. It was pure and basic financial desperation. It was all about money.

Three proprietors were granted Township Three, as Gouldsboro was originally designated. These were Nathan Jones, Francis Shaw and Robert Gould. They were men of means in and near Boston. Their title to Number Three had little to do with idealism or theology. It was pure investment. It was all about money.

The Revolutionary War did extensive damage to the fledgling economy in Gouldsboro which was based on lumber. The settlers, already poor,, were close to destitution. The proprietors were largely ruined. The government of Massachusetts was nearly ruined as well. Nathan Jones, youngest and last of the original proprietors, lived in

Jones's Quarter in quiet and comfortable possession, inhabiting the town he had helped to create. Robert Gould, Boston merchant, was heavily in debt to the English mercantile firm of Lane, Son and Fraser which itself was foundering because of huge American credit unredeemed during and after the war. Gould's firm failed and he died. Francis Shaw likewise died. The heirs of Shaw and Gould determined to sell the Gouldsboro lands if possible.

Massachusetts had an economic advantage in huge untapped assets, namely millions of acres of virgin land in the District of Maine. It was decided, after land lottery efforts had failed, that two large tracts should be sold to recoup badly needed income and offsetting the damaging costs of the war. A successful buyer eventually appeared in the person of William Bingham, wealthy merchant of Philadelphia. *[See the map and lottery ticket in Chapter Five.]*

Bingham wanted to invest in land. Huge tracts in Ohio, Pennsylvania and New York came into his ownership. Binghamton, New York reflects that ownership. Bingham became aware of the Massachusetts offer of wild land and negotiated the purchase of two large tracts of about a million acres each. These were the Kennebec Purchase in inland Maine near present day Skowhegan, and the Penobscot Purchase east of that river.

Commerce and income depended on water transportation. The Kennebec River provided access to the sea for Bingham's western purchase. In eastern Maine, however, the townships along the coast had been claimed by buyers from Massachusetts proper, and were already being settled. Thus, in the Penobscot Purchase, Bingham was denied an access to the sea. His eye fell upon Gouldsboro. It lay directly below and adjacent to his purchased eastern townships. *[See the map of eastern Bingham lands in Chapter Five.]* It could provide access to the sea. There had been only three proprietors. Thus he was able to negotiate with the heirs of Shaw and Gould to purchase the three quarters shares, not including settlers' lots of those already in place, not owned by Nathan Jones. Good anchorage was available in Gouldsboro Bay. On Gouldsboro Point Bingham intended to create a port city through which commerce of lumber from the inner million acres could be brought to the sea for distribution to markets, and goods and services be made available to inland settlers.

Yet Bingham himself, however vastly rich, was also feeling the pinch of the economic difficulties of the post-war time. He had already expended huge amounts for land in other places. He needed financial

support. His eye turned to England, to the international financial firm of Baring and Company. In Paris, the Duc de Richelieu later summarized the company's influence: "There are six main powers in Europe," the duke said, "Britain, France, Austria-Hungary, Russia, Prussia and the Baring Brothers." Sir Francis Baring, interested in developing investments in the New World, agreed to cooperate in Bingham's purchase. Neither Bingham nor Baring would live in Gouldsboro, so each appointed an agent to be on site and to represent them in the administration and development of the new property. It was all about money.

Now enters the person of Alexander Baring. Born 27 October 1774, he was infant and child during the years of the American war. He was brought up in his father's banking business and was, at a young age, sent to work for the continental banking institution of Hope and Company. This company owned the Hope Diamond, whence the gem derives its name, and was massively influential in European finance. One of Alexander Baring's sisters would marry Pierre Labouchere, one of the leading financiers of the company. Baring's Bank recognized in the former British colonies fresh and potentially great financial investments in the young and developing country. It was natural that they should join with William Bingham, reputed to be the wealthiest man in America. It was a marriage made of money.

General Henry Knox, close friend and military colleague of George Washington and resident owner of the Waldo Patent on the central Maine coast, observed that "no part of the United States affords such solid grounds of profits to capitalists as the District of Maine." So in the summer of 1795 Alexander Baring, aged twenty one, was

appointed emissary from his father in the massive venture with Bingham. The quality and future promise of the young man was expressed by Sir Francis. "I have a perfect confidence in his prudence, discretion and judgement." His task was to visit and survey the whole of the Bingham lands in Maine and recommend investment by Baring's – or not. In this way, Gouldsboro was seen – not as we see it in the forefront of our interest – but in the total context of the entire Bingham investment.

Bingham's view of the settler population in Gouldsboro is clearly stated. He speaks of "the state of society . . . existing on the seashore, where by the great profits of lumbering and fishing the lower classes of people who are usually employed in these pursuits have possessed the means of leading a life of comparative indolence which in that order of the community is usually accompanied by the debauchery and dissipation. Hence the reputation of the country was injured by the apparent poverty of these people, which necessarily arose from their profligate and idle course of life."

Alexander Baring arrived in Boston in November 1795. After planning and conferring with Bingham and Cobb, the party at last set out to explore Maine in June 1796. His assessment of Gouldsboro was not promising.

At Gouldsboro we found General Cobb, who accompanied us in all our excursions after wards. Gouldsboro' being the first part of the purchase we were to see . . . we were looking forward to it with great impatience, and I must confess the approach to it made me feel very unpleasantly indeed. The whole of the point is a white rock which presents the most barren object you can imagine and to add to the uncouthness of the scene, some pine woods had been burnt behind it, as is customary in clearing lands, which presented a singular contrast of white and black. Upon going farther back we found good land, but the point itself is fit for nothing but a town, for which it is in every respect situated. If any part of the country fell short of my expectations, it was certainly Gouldsboro . . . I could have wished it had not looked so frightfully barren . . . . I had rather expected to find more of a town and houses in better condition . . . there are not above three comfortable houses in it. Bingham was certainly deceived in his purchases there . . . . I have no doubt that this will in time become an important place. The country back is fine and the harbour very good, but more on account of its easy access and good anchoring than depth of water. This circumstance makes it a very convenient resort for the Bank fishing, which begins within sight of that part of the coast. In other parts of the township of Gouldsboro' there are good farms, and particularly round the inlet of water [West Bay] touching the corner of [inland township] No. 7. We staid on our first visit but a short time at Gouldsboro.

> *The network of financial alliances and marriages in three prominent families is diagramed below. It shows how heavy investment was brought to bear on the early development of Gouldsboro through the Bingham proprietorship. It was these connections and marriages that resulted in the arrival in Gouldsboro of its two most influential land agents, General David Cobb and John Black.*

THE GREAT INVESTORS IN GOULDSBORO

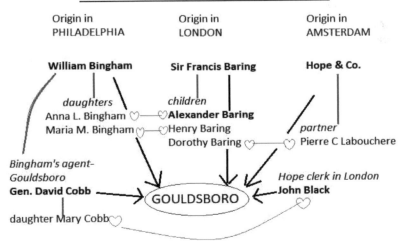

In 1797, coming up from Down East, Baring was back again. The evaluation was mostly unchanged.

From St John's we sailed to Passamaquoddy and from thence to Gouldsboro. . . . The neighborhood of the latter place . . . is by far the least promising in appearance of any part of our tract, indeed so much so that we have our doubts whether we should not remove our capitol elsewhere. Gouldsboro' has advantages of goodness of harbour and central situation beyond any other place, but its ragged appearance is a serious objection in a country where we want principally to introduce farmers.

In February 1798 Baring outlined in detail plans for the development of the Purchase. Part of this planning included the arrival of John Black. He was discovered by William Bingham in Hope and Company where he was working as a clerk, and was hired as agent to work with General Cobb in Gouldsboro. He arrived in 1799 at the age of eighteen. Alexander Baring described him as "a very steady young man [who] will be of great assistance in the office . . . you will find him very generally useful." Another of the plans involved a small ship, a packet, to carry mail and goods to and from Boston. "It should be a smart small vessel, I think a schooner, with tolerable accommodations of a common kind for passengers. It should be neatly painted on the outside and have *Gouldsborough Packet* in large letters on her stern. [It] will make Gouldsboro' the port of communication for the country east of Penobscot with Boston . . . bringing down passengers at a moderate passage money and returning with lumber." He continues with an evaluation somewhat revised:

> After much consideration of the advantages and disadvantages of Gouldsbro' [sic], I believe it must be our headquarters on the coast. The goodness of the harbour must insure its future importance tho' its dreary appearance makes it unfavorable for the first introduction of settlers . . . When the interior of the country is settled the poor appearance of Gouldsbro' Point will make no impression but its advantages as a harbor will secure it settlement and trade . . . our buildings in Gouldsbro' should be kept in good repair . . . they should all be painted outside to look neat which would remove much of the horrors of the place."

Still, one other observation of Gouldsboro is at some variance with Baring's earlier observations.

> From General Cobb's [on Gouldsboro Point] we crossed the township to the inlet on the other side, which is a peninsula. . . . Here we found . . . our vessel at anchor. On this inlet of water [Jones's Cove] lives the richest character east of Penobscot, a

▢ Colonel Jones . . . He owns the part of Gouldsboro' which does not belong to us and in fact the best part [West Gouldsboro]. He has long resided here, has a large farm, good house and three mills which go by water from a pond above him [Jones's Pond] which he lets through by sluices. He has been making experiments of all kinds and is useful to the country. As such, Cobb keeps friends with him and he received us very hospitably but we believe him to be a great rascal [*ie:* "a low, mean, unprincipled or dishonest fellow, a rogue, knave, scamp"] and do not trust him. The situation of his estate makes it not only remarkably beautiful and desirable but very valuable. He asks 30,000 for it and for a person who would live there it is worth that too but not to a speculator. Jones, who is an artful [*ie:* "cunning, crafty, deceitful"] man, having resided long in Maine, has picked up several of the most valuable spots and I believe has been cheating his neighbours, and especially the former proprietors of Gouldsboro' but for that there is no remedy and we can only take care of ourselves. He owns several vessels at sea, which he builds himself at his wharf; while we were there one of his ships returned from Europe on freight for her first voyage which had entirely paid her costs . . . . Frenchman's Bay . . . is a very good harbour and could contain the largest navy in safety, particularly on the Gouldsboro' side within the islands.

Baring's experience with Gouldsboro happened when he was a very young man, but his connections with American life and history were far from over. In August 1798, at the age of twenty four, Alexander Baring married William Bingham's daughter Anne Louisa,

*Alexander Baring, Lord Ashburton, signed the border dispute with Canada at his house in Washington DC, a building that later became the parish house (**at right**) of St. John's Episcopal Church, often called the "Church of the Presidents" for its proximity to the White House.*

aged sixteen, at "Bellevue," Bingham's summer home on the New Jersey coast. In 1802 her sister Maria married Sir Francis Baring's son Henry. In 1803 Alexander Baring engineered and financed the Louisiana Purchase for the United States. Sir Francis Baring the patriarch died in 1810 and the firm then became Baring Brothers and Co. The company acted as London bankers for the new Bank of the United States, whose president was Thomas Willing, father in law of William Bingham and grandfather of Anne Bingham Baring. It was all a matter of money.

Alexander Baring went on to become trustee of the British Museum and of the National Gallery in London. In private life he was one of the leading collectors of art in England and America. He was master of "The Grange" in Hampshire which is still owned by the Baring family. They are descendants of Alexander Baring and William Bingham, sometime owners of much of Gouldsboro. He was Master of the Mint and a member of the House of Commons in Parliament.

In 1835 he was raised to the English peerage as Alexander, 1st Baron Ashburton, and late in life, in 1842 at the age of sixty eight he was involved in one more American venture as representative of the British government in settling at last the boundary between the United States and Canada. The Aroostook War in Maine was fought over that issue. Daniel Webster and Lord Ashburton signed the final agreement at Ashburton House on Layette Square in Washington, D.C. where Lord Ashburton was living. The building is today the parish house for St John's Episcopal Church, called the Church of the Presidents.

Alexander Baring's life was varied and even colorful. Embedded in his international biography is little Gouldsboro, in company with Philadelphia, London and Amsterdam. It is a link connecting the town to the great world in America and beyond the sea, and long unrecognized.

Sources

*Oxford English Dictionary
*William Bingham's Maine Lands, (ed) Frederick S. Allis, Jr. in
    Publications of The Colonial Society of Massachusetts. Vol.
    XXXVI and XXXVII
*Ralph W. Hidy, The House of Baring in American Trade and Finance:
    English Merchant Bankers at Work 1763 – 1861.

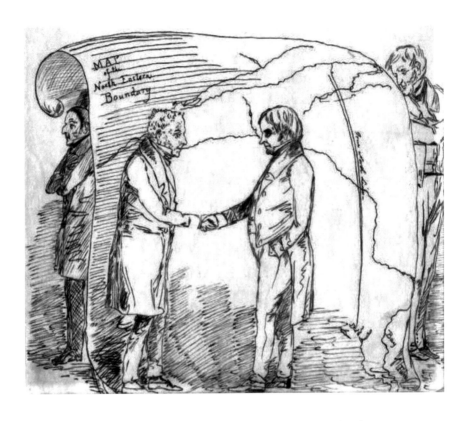

A cartoon showing Baring --as Lord Ashburton (left) -- settling a negotiated agreement with the U.S. Senator Daniel Webster (right), thus resolving the US- Canada boundary dispute and ending the "Aroostook War" of 1839. [Maine Historical Society}

Chapter 7

"A NEW FIELD of EXERTIONS": GENERAL COBB—LAND AGENT IN GOULDSBORO

General David Cobb is here shown in his later years when he played a major role in Massachusetts government and in Federalist politics. (Engraving from Joseph W. Porter, "Memoir of Gen. David Cobb...." in Sources below.)

The Rev. Joy in August of 2007 gave a version of this talk on Gouldsboro's first managing agent, General David Cobb. With his generous quotations from the journals of Cobb and others, we get an extraordinarily vivid view of daily life in the early settlement of Gouldsboro.

§

On 7 March 1795 in Philadelphia, David Cobb, a former general in the Revolutionary War, entered upon a second career at the age of forty seven. He was to become land agent and representative of William Bingham at Gouldsboro, in eastern Massachusetts in the District of Maine. Three days earlier he had walked with General Henry Knox "Conversing on the subject of Eastern Lands," and had dined with William Bingham. So, on the 7th he recorded that "The Eastern Land Agreement signed, which opens a new field of exertions for my abilities. Tho' untried I am determined to go thro'."

General Cobb badly needed a job. In 1791, it was said that David Cobb's situation was miserable and he had not a sixpence or other resource to provide for his family. The offer from William Bingham was important. As remuneration, he was to be deeded a lot in Gouldsboro and $1000 for the construction of a house. He was to receive a further 2000 acres in a place to be agreed upon. Profits from 20,000 acres of land were to go to him, and his cash salary was to be $1500 per annum beginning in May 1795. Cobb was a promising choice. Alexander Baring, writing to Henry Hope, observed "Method and system . . . Cobb does not [possess] but he is a very good man of an active mind, both for real execution and eminently for puffing [ie. publicizing] which his great influence in New England enables him to do with more effect than any other person."

David Cobb was born in Attleborough, Massachusetts in 1748, son of Thomas Cobb, a manufacturer of iron, and Lydia his wife. In 1760 the family moved to Taunton, Massachusetts where his father had a grist mill, a fulling mill and a rolling and slitting mill. Like John Adams, second president of the United States, David Cobb studied with Joseph Marsh who had graduated from Harvard in 1728. In 1762, at the age of fourteen, Cobb was admitted to Harvard College as a member of the class of 1766.

In the same year as his graduation Cobb married Eleanor Bradish, whose father was owner and keeper of the Blue Anchor Tavern in Cambridge, a favorite haunt of Harvard students. The couple would produce five daughters and four sons. He went on to study medicine with Dr Richard Perkins in Boston and went back to Taunton to practice. General Cobb's medicine box is seen today at Woodlawn, the museum that was built by his son-in-law John Black in Ellsworth.

Deeply involved in political and military leadership, David Cobb in 1774 became a member of the General Court, governing body of colonial Massachusetts. The next year he had a role in the Committee of Safety, Inspection and Correspondence as part of the pre-war organization in the colony. He served as surgeon in the army in Boston in 1776, before he was commissioned lieutenant colonel in 1777. From 1781 to the war's end he was aide de camp to General Washington and was beside the commander at the British surrender in Yorktown in October 1783. He left the army with the rank of brigadier general. It was a natural thing therefore, in the years following the war, for David Cobb to associate with the Federalist party of George Washington and others including General Henry Knox and William Bingham. Politics again became an activity of his life. He was made judge in the Court of Common Pleas in Bristol County at Taunton in 1784, and then in 1789, the year that Township Number Three was incorporated as Gouldsboro, he served again in the General Court and was its speaker for four years. He received honorary degrees from Princeton in 1783 and from Brown in 1790. Cobb was a founder of Bristol Academy, and was elected to the senate of the United States in 1793 where he would serve with William Bingham. Then he came to Maine.

Alexander Baring, who would become William Bingham's son in law, commented that "Bingham made a hard bargain with him . . . his services are in fact invaluable and no wonder he remains poor if he does not know how to rate them better." He felt Bingham had chosen his agent well, as a man with "the effort of mind necessary to conduct the enterprise as well as the interests of the proprietors to be eventually effected by its failure or success."

Baring outlined the immediate goals as, first, to obtain settlers, since "there is no [other] arrangement that can so easily tend to raise the value of these lands," and, second, to get possession of all the mill sites, which would prevent depredation of the timber resources and allow the Proprietor to "command the means of converting the wood into lumber."

After a six day sail from Boston in June 1795, Cobb arrived at Gouldsboro. He had arranged a team to begin the administration of the property. The surveyor was to receive a salary of $500 a year; six laborers were each to earn $10 to $12 per month; the housewright was to be paid $.75 per day and his board. Three or four of the laborers were to serve as chainmen to the surveyor in laying out accurate property lines and roads, and the remaining laborers were to work on the farms at Gouldsboro. First purchasers of land were to pay $.66 per acre, though the basic going price would be $1.00 per acre.

One of Cobb's missions was to command all available mill sites so as to "convert the wood into lumber" as Colonel Jones was already doing at this early mill site in West Gouldsboro. By November of 1796 Cobb was negotiating with Jones to take over a site that Jones had developed outside his claim, at Mill Stream in today's Winter Harbor. From there Cobb developed many other lumber mill sites. (Photo from Gouldsboro Historical Society)

What David Cobb found in Gouldsboro was daunting. "All was waste and ruin," he reported to Bingham, "not an enclosure . . . the finest marsh in this country a common pasture for the flocks [sheep] of the inhabitants, and your little houses occupied as sheepfolds." In the month of June, working in the woods, the surveyor and his coworkers "frequently returned almost blind by the bites of flies and mosketoes. . . . the hosts of these devils that infest the thick forest at this season." The farm laborers were busy making fences and "planting potatoes and other roots," and the housewright began building a dwelling for Cobb's family, who had not yet come from Taunton.

In August 1795 Cobb invited Henry Knox to come down the coast from his home in Thomaston to view the progress being made by

Bingham's new agent and his crew. "I shall surrender my room to Mrs Knox," he wrote, "and you and I (for we live here as they do in Heaven) with a blanket will sleep in the barn. The other ladies shall have the maid's room and she shall sleep with the hogs."

Henry Knox and David Cobb had much to share in addition to their common experience as officers in the Revolution. Knox, through marriage to the heiress of the colonial Waldo Patent, was a "Great Proprietor" on a scale only slightly less than Bingham, and had been experiencing similar problems administering land and property sales with unruly clients not unlike those in Gouldsboro. (Portrait of Knox by Charles Wilson Peale, National Portrait Gallery.)

One real step forward marking progress was the building of a schooner in Gouldsboro in that same summer of 1795. Fashioned "of the materials of this country, the top timbers and the plank of the waist with the knees are of larch [hackmatack] of which this country abounds, and which is perhaps as durable timber as any in America. The rest of the vessel is yallow [sic] birch, a very valuable timber."

Progress continued into the autumn as the laborers cut three miles of new road "north from this to the end of the Purchase." Meanwhile the house construction was going forward. A mason, two carpenters and two laborers were busy at the building. Had the road cutters been there instead of in the woods, Cobb reckoned, "we should be stowed as thick as herrings in a barrel." The greater challenge, however, was maintaining the estate assets in the acres of timberland belonging to Bingham. "Every inhabitant here is now a depredator – a trespasser – plunderer. They live by it and therefore will not cultivate the finest soil in the world." Yet Bingham, though remote from Gouldsboro and wealthy, was not heartless. "Such are the customs and habits of the people here" he wrote to Cobb, "that if they are denied the privilege of log cutting upon these lands they would be reduced to the utmost distress and out of charity to this necessity the Proprietor consents to their having this privilege on the following conditions." These conditions were that no trees fit for masts might be cut. One eighth of the boards cut from the timber at the mills was to be the fee, and if other timber is taken they must pay the "customary proportion."

In January 1796, David Cobb and Alexander Baring travelled together from Gouldsboro to Philadelphia to meet with William Bingham. Baring reported his assessment of General Cobb's personality. "Cobb and Knox are known all over the country. It would be impossible to get two other men so respected . . . . Cobb is one of those men who with a vast sum of good sense and more of humor have never been able to get forward in the world, and as he has a family, now thinks of providing for them in this manner . . . . Cobb's most valuable qualities to us are his character which is universally respected among the people we want to attract, and a suavity and pleasantry of manner exactly suited to manage them, for they will not be driven. The only thing I fear of his character is that, accustomed to the gay life, he will get tired of his farm."

By spring 1796 David Cobb was ready to move his family to the house newly built at Gouldsboro Point. In April and May a fever left him "sick in bed at Taunton," but on 19 May "I broke up housekeeping at Taunton, sent my furniture and stores on board of a vessel lying in the River [Taunton River] bound to Gouldsboro which sailed the day following." From mid-May to mid-June he was in Boston and Cambridge "looking for an opportunity for a conveyance for myself and family to Gouldsboro." Finally on 18 June they sailed from Boston, "passed Cape Ann at sun setting." The women and his little son were seasick on the sail down the coast to Maine.

Records of summer and fall in 1796 reveal activities and outlook of General Cobb that provide a cameo picture of his Gouldsboro life through twenty five years. The summer weather was largely foggy and rainy, in the discomfort of which they were working on "damned" fences to contain the precious livestock. Food was plentiful. Potatoes and beans were available from their garden; they went fishing and caught tom cods and flounders which they ate with clams they had dug. Accompanied by "old Mr Gubtail" who managed the mill at West Bay, Cobb went up the Guzzle trouting and "caught a dozen of the finest I ever see." In mid-July they began haying and made six tons to feed the animals in the long winter ahead. The roads were "infamous" and "infernal." Cobb wrenched his back during road building, and when he went to Machias he went by canoe.

A major trip at the end of July took David Cobb to visit General Knox at Thomaston. Colonel Jones was to provide him with the boat for the journey, but as that boat had been sent on an errand by Jones, they stayed at West Gouldsboro with the colonel for three days till it returned. The sail up the coast required three days. They landed at Camden and took horses, arriving at Knox's at night. The travelers, weary with the rather difficult sail, were "very happy in being under the Roof of a hospitable friend after five days vexation in constant fog and calm."

The house built for David Cobb and his family at "Fish Point" is shown in this rendition of a sketch perhaps preserved by his son-in-law John Black (later copied from the Black mansion by Leslie Charlette). The house was said to be situated on what was later the Whitaker family lot at Gouldsboro Point--at approximately the corner of today's Old County Road and Gouldsboro Point Road, near the Narrows and the landing. Note the masts of Cobb's new schooner moored nearby. (Image from Gouldsboro Historical Society)

August in the height of summer was busy in many activities involved with the laborious toil in creating a new town. In the close and high summer temperature, the surveyor and his chainmen, laying out new roads, all fell ill with heat stroke. Ground was being cleared for rye and wheat. By month's end they had cleared eight acres, using oxen to haul burned and blackened logs from the newly opened spaces and piled them with roots to create fences. Cobb called it "delightful work tho' very dirty." It very nearly spelled disaster. "I am so fond of this business that I foolishly engaged with the black logs myself, the sudden rolling of one of which came within an ace of breaking my thigh. I took this for a caution and quitted the work black enough." The table was provided with beans, cucumbers and peas coming in from the garden.

The turn of seasons was clear in September "Preparing the Fall work." More than a week was spent in his attendance on court in the then county seat at Castine, requiring two days each way to go and come. On 24 September came the first frost which killed beans, potatoes and cucumbers. Jonathan Tracy provided Cobb with a pig and a yoke of young oxen. When these oxen jumped their fence at night, two days' search was required to retrieve them. Less than a week later, they again escaped "and are gone off, I hope to the Devil." Ploughing to prepare the fields for winter was under way as days shortened and cold weather came on. Chimneys were being built in the company store and the Cobb house, which he called his "Nest," and on the last day of the month "family removed to neighbor Godfrey's where we cook our food but we still lodge in our rooms, however disagreeable, it must be submitted to till chimney is finished."

October presented a variety of difficulties for the General. Early in the month, returning home from Machias, he was fording the Chandler River eight miles west of Machias. He related to William Bingham the nearly disastrous event. "The rapidity of the current trip'd my horse and swept me down the river. My little art of swimming, which I have not exercis'd for fifteen years before, enabled me to reach the shore, twelve rods below [nearly two hundred feet], altho' incumber'd with my great coat, but so exhausted as to be incapable of rising for some minutes. I escaped, thank God, with only the rheumatism for which I am now cloath'd in flannel." Cobb described the experience to Knox as "my escape from seeing our friends in the other world."

He was responsible for a large number of people. "My family at present large enough: seven Road Cutters and Col. Hall their Commander with Mr Peters the Surveyor, all of whom encamp in the Woods, two Masons, two Carpenters and ten Labourers at the House, besides Mr Tillinghast, myself, two sons and two Maids."

The road cutters had cleared about seven miles in the northerly direction. They "have a very good Hutt which being covered with branches now shelters them from all weather." Cobb carried them their dinner every day and ate with them. Once the cutters, heading for their hut, stopped at a neighboring house and, with the owner of the house, drank up three days' provision of rum and stayed there drunk all night. At this the General flashed a temper and gave a tongue lashing that years earlier had been used to control troops. "I told them when they applied to go home that they might go, and welcome, for I wished to have no dealings with a set of deceiving,

87

COL. JONES QUARTER

Public Lot

West Bay

Gouldsboro Point

Public Lot

Prospect Bay

Public Lot

Schoodic Point

LOTS SURVEYED FOR

WILLIAM BINGHAM

1798

and sold
by his agents
in later years

Part of Cobb's responsibility was to promote respect for a new set of property bounds in Gouldsboro, and to administer sales for Bingham land. Some of these plots had previously been sold to earlier settlers, especially around West Bay, Gouldsboro Point, and Prospect Harbor, but the remainder-- **all of the dark area** lots shown in this map-- were for sale by Bingham's agent, General Cobb and his successors. [Map byThomas Mayer]

drunken, mischief making rascals, and I would pay them nothing for what they had done, and I would prosecute them for damages in not complying with the terms of their engagement when their sickness was feigned, and I would not be imposed upon by such scoundrels. . . . [T]o those who complained of being unwell I told them they were deceiving villains." Next day, recovered, they begged forgiveness and "they returned to their work in the Woods." Clearly they were duly chastened. Still, he had a certain amount of humor on the subject. "Rum and the waters of this country are the only avenues the people have to the other world. But for these and a little old age the inhabitants would be immortal for they have no diseases."

In November, with winter in the offing, the work season was winding up. Carrying pork, "biskitts," and a bottle of brandy, Cobb went to inspect the route laid out for the new road. Camping near a falls, they made huts of bushes with a large fire at their feet (apparently no fear that the huts would be incinerated), and, with the brandy as a soporific, "we slept comfortably in our Great Coats during the night." Later they were joined by several guests and ate boiled and fried codfish and some "good Port." The work in the woods was left off for the season and the twelve road cutters were set to work clearing the newly made mowing ground of stones and pulling up the stumps with teams of oxen. As he began the long sail westward to Boston, on 21 November at Blue Hill he was "reflecting upon the state in which I had left my Gouldsboro concerns. I am rather pleased with the review." On 1 December David Cobb was reunited with his family at Taunton "after an absence of more than six months."

With this auspicious beginning, General Cobb went on to provide a vital and urgent stability to a fractured and insecure settlement during a time of great uncertainty when even the form of the government of the new nation was uncertain. The significant length of time of his work in Gouldsboro, his daily attention to detail, his hands-on involvement in the town's development and government, and at his final retirement to Massachusetts, leaving his talented son-

In his later years as Bingham's Gouldsboro agent, Cobb spent much of his time serving as Judge, Senator, and Lieutenant Governor at the 1798 Massachusetts State House, here shown in an early engraving. Thus he expanded his influence into the state's Federalist government and as Gouldsboro's man in Boston.

in-law John Black as agent, all contributed to his significance in the town's life and history. His presence and active attention to the many facets of the Bingham agency made a greatly needed transition, a bridge from the initial time of settlement, of war and of disruption, into a more stable economic and political climate in the Nineteenth Century. While Cobb's vision of a basically agricultural way of life became only partly true, during his years in the agency Gouldsboro moved from the original extractive economy of lumbering to a larger dependence on fishing and the sea.

William Bingham died at Bath in England in 1804. Cobb continued under Bingham's trustees what had become the rather daunting work of agent. In April 1808 he noted that "a severe Lumbago has confined me to my house for nearly three months . . . peculiarly distressing," but with unvarnished optimism he noted "I am now however returned to my usual health and hope the warm weather will thoroughly thaw me out."

The trustees of the Bingham estate decided at length to remove all Bingham's agents. In the summer of 1820, David Cobb wrote: "I am very infirm, but at seventy two we ought not to complain; I am so unwell at present as scarcely to hold my pen." His handwriting had deteriorated as years had passed, and the infirmity was visible in quavering penmanship.   In 1820 the District of Maine became independent of Massachusetts, entering the Union as a free state balancing Missouri, a slave state. Cobb returned permanently to Taunton, his childhood home. He had lived in Maine as Bingham's agent for twenty five years. In that time, he had served as Chief Justice of the Court of Common Pleas for Hancock County from 1803 to 1809, senator in the General Court of Massachusetts from 1801 to 1804, and Lieutenant Governor of Massachusetts in 1809. In 1825, at the age of seventy, in Boston he greeted the venerable Marquis de Lafayette on his final visit to America.   One could wish their conversation had been preserved.

He died 17 April 1830 in the Massachusetts General Hospital in Boston.   Among the encomia appearing in his praise, one perhaps most succinctly captured the personality of a man who was, in many senses, for a quarter century the leading citizen of Gouldsboro:

> Whenever he appeared at the social board his wit and humor, his fund of anecdote and power of pleasing gave zest. [He] was not free from faults, but his faults left no stings of remorse . . . [He was] a politician without deceit, a statesman without ambition, a patriot without violence, and a warrior without ferocity . . . . Age had neither chilled his blood nor frozen his heart.

Sources

*William Bingham's Maine Lands, (ed) Frederick S. Allis, Jr in Publications of the Colonial Society of Massachusetts, Vol. XXXVI and CCCVII

*Clark, Grace Wood. *Historical Researches of Gouldsboro, Maine.* Gouldsboro: Daughters of Liberty, 1904.

*Baylies, Hon. Francis. "Some Remarks on the Life And Character of General David Cobb, Delivered at the Taunton Lyceum, July 2nd 1830. *New England Historic Genealogical Register,* January 1864.

*Kennedy, Edward F., Jr. *David Cobb An American Patriot.* Taunton, Mass.: Old Colony Historical Society, 1982.

*Porter, J. W. "Memoir of General David Cobb and Family, of Gouldsborough, Maine, and Taunton, Mass." *Bangor Historical Magazine,* July – August 1883 (IV/1 and 2), reprinted Camden, Maine: Picton Press, 1993, p.725 ff.

Chapter 8

COLONEL JOHN BLACK: AN UNSUNG STORY

This portrait of John Black in his later years hangs in his Ellsworth mansion and is property of the Woodlawn Museum, an institution devoted to the city's cultural and historical traditions. (Woodlawn Museum)

Here a summary of Gouldsboro's founding leads into Rev. Joy's account of John Black, a leader whose career formed a bridge from the town's proprietors to its early development in the first half of the 19th Century. This talk was given in August of 2015.

℘

One of the cultural attractions and tourist centers of Down East Maine is Woodlawn, often called "the Black House," in Ellsworth. Ellsworth proudly and rightly claims it as a place of local importance for its history and for its culture. It has become a center of community activities of many kinds.

Unspoken and unrealized, however, is how the house and its builder, Colonel John Black (1781 – 1856) have important links with Gouldsboro. The house was the creation and home, until his death, of a man who played a key role in the history and development of Gouldsboro. Nothing happens in a vacuum. To understand his unrecognized role of importance in Gouldsboro's life and growth, it is important to see the context from which he emerged and in which he played his part.

Geography is the stage upon which the drama of history happens. In order to understand this man and the role he acted in Gouldsboro's story, the story of the land itself must be understood. There are five layers or levels in which land development took place.

The first level has to do with the Indians and the French. Until 1763 the Penobscot River was the boundary between two European empires: British New England and French Canada. The largely empty territory east of that river was in title French but inhabited principally by Indian tribes. The French and Indian War – also known as the Seven Years War – ended, at the signing of the Peace of Paris in February 1763. Britain had emerged the victor. In this way the French domination ended, and thus, so far away, began the Anglo-Saxon history of eastern Maine, whose lands were ultimately assigned to the colony of Massachusetts.

The second level of development is the British colonial period. British settlers began to leak into the newly acquired territories in a more or less haphazard way, led by people known as "squatters," who were little concerned with legal title but primarily with escaping the desperation of poverty. They were people of English descent mostly originating in New Hampshire and western Maine. Jonathan Tracy (1713 – 1796) and his wife Abigail were among the first. Born in

Connecticut, he was a saddle maker living most recently in Falmouth, Maine.

Massachusetts lost little time in beginning to organize their newly acquired lands. This "eastern territory" was surveyed for the government of the Massachusetts colony and in 1764 six townships along the coast east of Union River were laid off and granted to proprietors. (*See the maps in Chapter Five.*) They were laid out in a grid, made irregular by the contour of the coastline. One had fifty one proprietors, one had fifty eight, three had sixty. Unusually, Gouldsboro, in a very distinctive way, was assigned to only three men. They were Robert Gould, Boston merchant who gave his name to the new settlement; Nathan Jones, son of a prominent member of the colonial legislature, and Francis Shaw, a businessman in Boston.

The John Black house, now the Woodlawn Museum in Ellsworth, Maine, was a crowning architectural achievement for Black as agent for the Bingham properties. He had moved his center of operations to Ellsworth as early as 1809 but did not build the mansion until the 1820s, moving into it with his family in 1828. (Library of Congress)

Scarcely ten years on, the Revolutionary War erupted. Gouldsboro was a subsistence colony depending for its economy on lumber shipped to Boston. The war, and the British blockade in the Gulf of Maine, interrupted the economy. Nathan Jones owned one quarter of the township. Gould had died. Thomas Lane, to whom much had been mortgaged, was ruined by the war. The titles to three quarters of the township came, in a very complex way, to William Shaw. In line with legislation in Massachusetts he legalized the settlement rights of many of the squatters who received 100 acres each. So in the 1790s, Gouldsboro was ready for what was coming next.

The third level of development involved a new proprietor. He was William Bingham (1752 – 1804), wealthy merchant in Philadelphia and friend of George Washington. Following great expenses in prosecuting the war, Massachusetts found itself low on money. Yet it held a major potential commodity: untold virgin acres "at the eastward" in the Maine lands, which had been part of Massachusetts since 1652. Two million acres were bought by Bingham. Binghamton, New York, was named for him in vast tracts that he held in that state.

In Maine Bingham bought two parcels: the Kennebec Purchase in the headwaters of that river, and the Penobscot Purchase in Hancock and Washington Counties. His goal was investment and development, but in order to prosper he needed an outlet to the sea. His landlocked parcel required a seaport for shipping, for the development of agriculture, and as a commercial center. Gouldsboro was the logical choice. He bought the three quarters of the township belonging to William Shaw, minus the various settlers whose titles had been cleared under the law. (*See the maps in Chapter5.*) In all, the Gouldsboro purchase came to 7393 acres. Gouldsboro Harbor and Gouldsboro Point were his focus of development. The sale was completed in 1795.

The fourth level of development now began to take shape. Bingham needed an able and decisive hands-on manager in place in the settlement who could oversee the work in a close fashion. General David Cobb (1748 – 1830) was a Revolutionary officer and General Washington's aide-de-camp, and widely known in Federalist circles. He came from Taunton, Massachusetts to Gouldsboro in 1795 as Bingham's on the ground agent, and lived in the town until 1820. Bingham, though wealthy, was backed in his massive enterprise by Barings Bank in London. Alexander Baring, Lord Ashburton, was Bingham's son in law. Baring's agent was a young Englishman, John

Richards, who left his home in Hampshire, England and came to Gouldsboro working with General Cobb to represent the interests of the bank. (*See the diagram of these relationships in Chapter Six.*)

The fifth level of development now opens. In London through the Barings John Richards met a young accountant in the employ of Hope and Company, bankers in Holland and England. The accountant's name was John Black. He was hired to come to Gouldsboro and work with Cobb in the administration and oversight of the enterprise of Bingham and Baring.

Little is known of his early life. He was born, by his own statement, on 3 July 1781 at Whitehaven in Cumberland, in the north of England. His parents were John Black, a shoemaker, and Ann Nixon who had been married in Rockcliffe, the small village where Ann was born. It is four miles from the cathedral city of Carlisle which was, as it were, the Ellsworth/Bangor of Black's earliest years.

Before Black's family moved to London they were in the border district of Cumbria and the city of Carlisle or its surrounding villages, where John Black was born and grew up. (View of Carlisle in the 1700s: Engraving, National Library of Scotland)

The family included two younger sisters, Elizabeth and Harriet Stewart Black, born in 1787 and 1792 in Wigtownshire, Scotland, where perhaps their father had originated. Very soon the family moved to London, the great urban mecca, and John Black was apprenticed to the banking house of Hope and Company to learn the accounting trade. So it was that at the age of seventeen he was chosen to go with John Richards to Gouldsboro.

John Black was clearly bright and talented, and he quickly rose to some prominence. He became naturalized as an American citizen. From 1805 he served as an officer in the Gouldsboro militia, and in that service as a Lieutenant Colonel he served in Mount Desert in the War of 1812. By war's end he obtained the rank of Colonel. In addition, during the time of his Gouldsboro residency, he served as town clerk and justice of the peace.

In 1802 he married Mary Cobb, the boss's daughter. He was twenty one and she was twenty six. Their first four of eight children – Mary Ann, John, Henry, and Elizabeth – were born in Gouldsboro between 1803 and 1809. In 1809 John Black purchased for $1 per acre two lots of land in Gouldsboro one comprising 140 acres and the other 1041 acres, from the Bingham estate. He received title to the lots on 26 July and on 1 August he conveyed both lots to his father in law General Cobb.

Clearly John Black was spreading his wings and contemplating a move to Ellsworth. In the same month as the deeds to Cobb, on 12 August 1809 "John Black of Gouldsborough, Gentleman," bought for $400 land "lying now in Ellsworth in that part set off from the town of Surry . . . on Union River. This would prove to be the first of multitudes of his land transactions in years to come. General Cobb returned to Taunton, where he had been born, in 1820. In 1824 his son in law John Black became agent in all of Maine for the Bingham proprietary.

One might see this as the end of the Gouldsboro chapter of John Black's life, but the connection with the town was to continue strongly – and even affectionately – until his death. Gouldsboro needed its own sub-agent. The titles and distribution of legalized settlers' lots sold by William Shaw preceding the sale to Bingham were complex and scattered over the more than 7000 acres of the Bingham lands in the town. (*See the maps in Chapter Seven.*) None of this, it should be remembered, was in the quarter owned by the original proprietor Nathan Jones in Jones's Quarter. The complexity of titles and irregular distribution of lots required an in-house agent. When General Cobb retired to Taunton in 1820 he was succeeded as agent by his son Thomas Cobb, John Black's brother in law.

Gouldsboro had been bought to become the gateway to the sea for the "Penobscot Million" which lay inland behind the seashore townships laid off by the colonial government in 1764. Gouldsboro with its harbor was to become a sort of capitol for the Bingham lands. On 22 January 1828 from his home in Ellsworth, Colonel Black addressed a letter to "Mr Wales Taft in Gouldsboro. "I have had it in contemplation to offer you the agency of those lands that Thos. Cobb Esq. has had the superintendence of for several years. . . . therefore if you are pleased to accept the appointment, you may consider yourself authorized to act for me in capacity of agent." So began a relationship that would last until John Black's death.

Black had far-flung responsibility for both the Penobscot Million and the Kennebec Million, and he reported directly to the Trustees of the Estate of William Bingham in Philadelphia.. In Ben Ames Williams's novel *The Strange Woman,* John Black plays a role. The author observed, in the words of one of the characters, "Colonel Black thinks of townships as other men think of acres. It's like managing a kingdom." The long series of letters from Black to Taft, found in the letter books in the Black papers, reveal what was involved in terms of the agency in Gouldsboro of which Ephraim Wales Taft was appointed head.

By moving operations to Ellsworth around 1809, John Black attached himself to a growing center of commercial activity. Even before Black built his own mansion, the town's prosperous merchants had built impressive homes such as this Federalist-style building built in 1817 for Colonel Meltiah Jordan. The house has been a public library since 1897 when Black's son George Nixon Black gave the remodeled building to the City of Ellsworth for library use. (Library of Congress)

There were three large basic principles of the operation of the agency of the Bingham estate in Gouldsboro. The first was that the land was intended ultimately to be divided into lots and sold. The purchases of William Bingham were investment property. The sale price and the process of sale were always carried on by John Black. When the property was sold, it was always in the name of "the Heirs of William Bingham."

The second principle of operation was that, until sold, the land had to be administered; land taxes had to be paid to town, county and state; its assets guarded until times of sale. Timber and wood products could be reaped with proper supervision by Wales Taft, and the appropriate monies collected. The process for this harvesting involved applying for and receiving a written permit to cut on specified Bingham lots and evaluating "stumpage," the numbers of trees cut on a particular piece of land. The agreed amount of money for each tree cut was called "rent" for the land use. These activities were overseen by Ephraim Wales Taft as agent in Gouldsboro, and reported to Colonel Black.

The third principle of the agency operation had to do with the not infrequent issue of "trespass." These were frequent and many. It fell to the local agent to analyze and evaluate the amount of trespassing on the resources of the estate, and then to recoup the value of the depredations. In some cases, the cut timber itself, or the sawn lumber, would be confiscated and marked. "Rent"

Busy as he was administering the vast Bingham holdings in Eastern Maine, Black needed an agent to manage the Bingham properties that lay in Gouldsboro. He was fortunate in finding Ephraim Wales Taft (shown here)— a steady and influential townsman who could responsibly protect these lots and sell them.
[Collection of C.A.Joy]

needed to be retrieved for the stumpage. In the event that no concurrence was to be had from the trespassers, there would issue a court suit at Castine, seat of Hancock County, or at Ellsworth when the seat was moved. Suits would be heard and adjudged in the Court of Common Pleas, and the Bingham interest would be represented in the courtroom by Taft as local agent.

All of these actions involved money, for which careful accounts were maintained by Taft in his ledger, in the account named for John Black. In the sometimes elaborate activities in Gouldsboro Ephraim Wales Taft and John Black were working colleagues and companions for nearly thirty years. The accounts in the Great Ledger for the work as agent are always headed "In account with John Black."

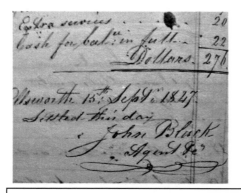 

Black and Taft were in regular communication about the management of Bingham's lands in Gouldsboro. Accounts were kept between them to bill for maintenance expenses, both in Taft's ledger and in Black's records, both shown in this listing of items during the 1840s. [Collection of C.A.Joy]

Just following his death, "in the autumnal era of a life of honored usefulness," Colonel Black's career and contributions, and the scope of his responsibilities, were aptly summarized in "Biographical Notice of Col. John Black":

For nearly sixty years Col. Black was identified with the management of the Bingham lands. . . . In the leasing of these lands to lumbering operations, -- in the sale of portions to actual settlers upon them, -- the opening and building the great roads, known so long and so famously by his name, through many of the townships in his charge, -- in encouraging and promoting by various ways a settlement upon them, and in disposing of the millions of acres under his supervision at prices which,, while remunerating to the Proprietary, were not exorbitant to the adventurous purchaser; in all this, the policy of Col. B was one of marked liberality without waywardness; but with a judgement ever considerate, uniform, just and delicate, he met the multifarious and conflicting interests of communities and individuals; while high or low,rich or poor, were sure to find in him a patient and heedful listener for the story of their misfortunes and disappointments.

John and Mary Black were the parents of eight children. Their son George Nixon Black would succeed him as agent for the Bingham heirs. The Colonel at his death held widespread personal investments in land and business. These interests included columns of deeds bought and sold in his own name apart from the Proprietary, mills, manufacture of lumber and ship building.

In the last seven years of his life his biographer noted that his sight failed. "Col. Black met with a severe misfortune in the loss of his sight. Accidentally discovering that one of his eyes had become so diseased by a cataract that its sight was completely destroyed, he consulted oculists who, deeming the operation safe, and success more than hopefully sure, undertook to remove it. For a few days after the operation there was every augury of success; but unfortunately a sympathetic inflammation attacked the other eye, and despite the best exertions, the sight of both was lost." On 9 October 1849, for the first time a letter to Ephraim Wales Taft was signed "John Black Agt. by G. N. Black." His wife Mary (Cobb) Black died in 1851 and the next year John married her niece Frances, who survived his death as his widow.

Black's estate was comprised of much real estate in Ellsworth, developed and undeveloped, stores, wharves and rental houses. His landholdings at the time of his death included land in the towns of Hancock and Waltham, 19,743 acres in Township 33, and another 1000 acres in Township 20. His total real estate holdings totaled $88,554 in value. His inventory also included $10,000 worth of shares in four vessels as well as many notes and mortgages. The total valuation of his estate was $230,265. The value becomes yet more striking in view of the fact that a man's basic salary was one dollar a day, giving rise to the expression "Another day, another dollar." His will included bequests to "my beloved sisters Eliza Mempriss and Mary Harriet Stewart Kerr," both living at 23 Prospect Place, Clapham, Surrey, in greater London. Bequests were made to Parker Institute for the Blind in Boston, and to the Maine Insane Hospital at Augusta where his tragic son Henry, born in Gouldsboro, was confined until his death.

People noted the personal qualities of Colonel John Black. He was said to be "short and thick of stature." He was a generous man, sometimes paying the taxes levied on the poor. He was meticulous in business, seemingly endless letter books and ledgers dealing with all the facets of his complex life. He was public spirited: in Gouldsboro he made two grants of land for the public use, for a wharf and for the Town House. Detailed as he was, he delegated authority; he did not micromanage, and trusted Ephraim Wales Taft to act dependably and faithfully in his stead to administer the agency of the Bingham estate in Gouldsboro. "He loved the country of his birth and the country of his adoption, regarding them as twin brothers, whose hands should be ever grasped in friendship," said his biographical notice. He was beneficent in his acts and in his thoughts. Oddly, Mary Black, John Black and George Nixon Black all died in the month of October.

Colonel Black's son George Nixon Black inherited Woodlawn House. Mrs. Black lived there until her death in 1874. George died there in 1880 and the estate was left to his only son George Nixon Black Jr., a resident of Boston. At his death in 1928 George Jr. bequeathed the Woodlawn estate and all the contents of the house to the Hancock County Trustees of Public Reservations. Today Woodlawn is a valuable and valued part of the Ellsworth scene, yet it is important as well to remember and honor the strong and unique ties that bind both the house and its builder to the town of Gouldsboro. They are part of the story of the town, centering in the remarkable figure of John Black, the shoemaker's son: an unsung story.

Sources

Ellsworth American issues:
  -5 December 1856, quoting
  "Biographical Notice of Col. John Black" in "Daily Whig & Courier."
  -7 October 1880.
  -12 – 26 August & 2 September 1993.
  -16 March 1995.
Bangor Historical Magazine May – October 1888
New England Historic Genealogical Register, October 1929, p. 470
*Diocese of Carlisle, England Marriage Bonds
*Black Papers: letter books, microfilm roll 28, Fogler Library, University of Maine.
*Town Records of Gouldsboro.
*Hancock County Deeds.
*Hancock County Probate, Files 2421 and 3972.

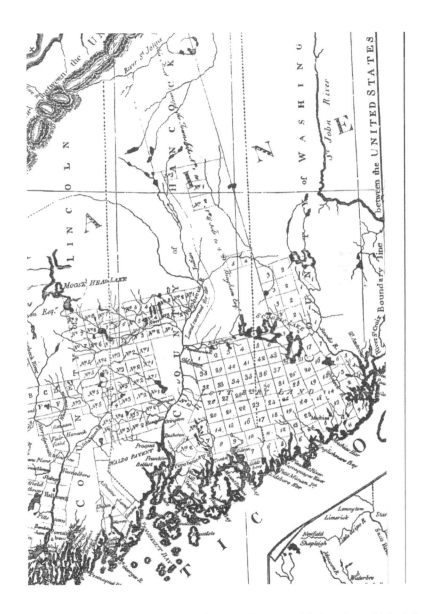

An early map of Bingham townships in Eastern Maine for which John Black was the agent in charge of land sales. [Library of Congress]

Chapter 9

OF WOODS AND WATER: EARLY ECONOMIES OF GOULDSBORO

Critical to Gouldsboro's economy was its maritime trade, and a key part of that was shipbuilding, primarily of two-masted vessels—brigs and schooners. Here the newly built schooner "Seth Nyman" is ready for launching in West Bay. [Photo: Gouldsboro Historical Society.]

This broad overview of Gouldsboro's changing economic development was delivered to the Historical Society in August of 2006. Here many of the concerns of the founders are shown coming together as the town slowly grew and diversified.

℘

Gilbert White (1720–1793), for many years curate of the parish of Selborne in Hampshire, England, is remembered as an observant and astute naturalist. On 20 October 1771 , he noted "mild and sun, a sweet day," though ominously there had been a "large halo round the moon," foretelling in that balmy autumn the approach of a seasonal storm. That storm arrived in full fury, and for 25 October he noted "white frost, sun, tempest. Vast rain and wind."

As Parson White, from the security of his rectory, dispassionately observed and recorded rather violent weather conditions, a small vessel from America was beating her way past Ireland. The *Diana*, fully laden with milled timber as cargo, was bound for London. The great storm struck as she was nearing the English coast. Driven off course in the sea winds, or perhaps because her master, Captain Peter Taylor, sought refuge from the open ocean in the Severn estuary, the *Diana* and her crew were driven ashore on Pickwell Sands in north Devonshire. The vessel foundered, with all hands lost, in the autumn gales and sea swells and surf of a massive storm. The register of Mortehoe Parish records the fate of the crew:

"A man found on Woolacombe Sands supposed to be a seaman was buried Oct. 27th 1771"

"A man found on Woolacombe Sands supposed to be a seaman was buried Oct. 30th 1771"

"A man found on Woolacombe Sands supposed to be a seaman was buried Nov. 7th 1771."

"All buried in Woolen only."

This catastrophe recalls T. S. Eliot's words in *The Dry Salvages:"* "You whose bodies suffer the trial and judgement of the sea." Why do we recall this ancient and forgotten disaster? The reason is provided by the reporting entry in a Boston newspaper. "A Brig belonging to this place, Taylor, Master, bound from Gouldsborough with a load of lumber, was cast away on Barnstable Bar in England, and the Vessel lost, and every Soul on Board perished." Lloyd's of London, the great insurance company, noted: "The *Diana*, Taylor, from Gouldsborough to

London, is lost off Barnstaple, and all the Crew perished." Woods and water: these are basic elements in the early economy of Gouldsboro. First lumber and the sea, then fishing and the sea, represent the lives of ordinary settlers and people in Gouldsboro, as opposed to the essential but mostly different lives of the proprietors. These – and others like them – were the people and the process of the daily labor that made real and sustained Gouldsboro's life.

The foundation of the settlers' economy, supporting all the rest of life, was lumber. The places of this maritime disaster – Gouldsboro, Boston and London – identify the basic dimensions of this earliest economy. The frontier village in the New World and the capital of the biggest empire reflect the scope and interconnected way of life that is also clearly seen in the lives of the proprietors. Trade was the lifeblood of the colonial system. This tiny place was a source of raw material; the British Empire was the market. Regardless of the personal aspirations of the settlers, from the beginning the British colonies up and down the coast of North America were settled and sustained for the wider growth and economy of the mother country. The sea was the highway. For the District of Maine, Boston was the filter and conduit through which trade passed.

The economic base was simple: lumber and other products of the forest. It was subsistence through an undifferentiated economic system, using what was at hand in the still uncut forests of the Gouldsboro peninsula. It was a crop that was not cultivated, but extracted. Gouldsboro was an eighteenth century mill town. Not only was it covered with an abundance of uncut wood in forests untouched time out of mind, but there was an eager market. Wood was the ubiquitous building material of the colony. In Boston even firewood was in short supply, and lumber in Britain was scarce. Perhaps today in some buildings on the Devon coast are pieces of lumber, grown in Gouldsboro earth, cut in Gouldsboro forests and sawn in Gouldsboro mills, that washed ashore with the bodies of drowned seamen on Pickwell Sands, and gathered by inhabitants of this English village to be incorporated into their buildings.

Gouldsboro in its earliest days was not a place of professional people. Early deeds record the presence of several trades: shipwright, millwright, mariner, blacksmith, tanner, saddle-maker, tailor and cordwainer. Supporting all the rest was lumber. Saw mills, appearing early, processed the raw material from the woodlands into finished products to be shipped away, like the cargo of the *Diana*. Saw mills were essential to process lumber from timber. Identified among the records are Whitten and Parritt's sawmill, referenced as early as 1772.

Wakefield's "new" mill stood on the stream that marked the boundary between Gouldsboro and Township Number Four (now Steuben) on the east, later called Whitten Parritt Stream. Four Bachelors Mill was gone by 1792, and Two Friends Mill came to be called Chicken Mill. Pinkham's Long Tide Mill was a double mill (that is grist mill and saw mill) on the west side of Gouldsboro Harbor at Indian Harbor (now Corea). The Upper Western Mill and Lower Western Mills were near the Guzzle. Saw mills called Upper and Lower Prospect Harbor Mills stood on the drain from Forbes Pond. There were mills on Fish Point Farm in Gouldsboro Point, and proprietor Nathan Jones had both a grist mill and a saw mill on the stream that drains Jones's Pond.

The market for lumber and wood products made it imperative for early Gouldsboro settlers to establish saw mills powered by local streams and tidal flowage. Colonel Nathan Jones established the original of this sawmill powered by the steam from Jones Pond in West Gouldsboro. [Photo: Gouldsboro Historical Society.]

The new settlement was only a decade or so old when the Revolution came. British ships interrupted trade that was the little settlement's lifeblood. In spring 1778 the town was reported to be "in a Deplorable Situation occasioned by the total Stagnation of the Lumber Trade, upon which we mostly depended for a living." That summer, in a kind of understatement, the settlers expressed "Disappointment in not being able to Dispose of a large Number of Masts, Sparrs &c" and therefore "unable to purchase anything for the

Reliefe of said Distressed Inhabitants." Besides lumber – pine boards and planks like the cargo of the *Diana* – the mills produced wood products for the building of vessels: spars, booms, keel pieces of oak and rock maple, masts seventy six to eighty feet long, and bowsprits. Timber was the commodity of the mill town. The sea was the trade lane. Ships were the transport vehicles.

The Revolutionary War knocked a mighty hole in a small economy; yet damaged as the lumber industry had been, the very location of Gouldsboro, with a good harbor on the sea, had great strategic potential. For the massive development envisioned by William Bingham for his 1795 Penobscot Purchase, he needed a port to open his million landlocked acres to the sea. With the purchase of all the unsettled land belonging to the Shaws, Bingham developed a wider vision than a simple lumber mill town. His agent David Cobb wrote, ". . . it is of first importance, that every exertion should be made . . . to establish every mechanical profession at Gouldsborough. . . and for making it the depot of the lumber of that country." Bingham himself articulated his ideal of development. "I have no doubt that in a short period, small, commercial establishments will be formed there [in Gouldsboro] which will give life and energy as well to the town as to the surrounding country and seashore, by purchasing fish, lumber and other productions, in exchange for groceries and imported articles."

By 1798 there were in the town six saw mills (value: $3940) and three grist mills (value: $1102). What had been an unbroken forest at the time of settlement had, by mid-nineteenth century, been fairly thoroughly cut over. In the spring of 1857, Ephraim Wales Taft (1795-1873) observed: "the lands in this town have been all burnt over or nearly all within a few years and there is nothing on the land now excepting a little old kiln wood. . . ."

By 1850, as lumber thinned, the economy of Gouldsboro had become more diversified. The range of work was much widened. The federal census of that year listed 325 jobs. Of these were listed sixty seven farmers—about 40%--, and carpenters and laborers listed at fifteen each, six each of joiners and lumbermen, four traders, three each of shoemakers and peddlers, two each of merchants, doctors and schoolteachers. There was one each listed for painter, clergy, blacksmith, harness maker and tailor. In addition, 59.6% followed maritime trades. These included seventy five seamen, seventy one fishermen, twenty two sailors, seven sea captains, three coasters, one whaler and fifteen ship carpenters.

One of the early fisheries in Prospect Harbor was local whaling, extracting the oil of eight or ten whales annually in large land-based try pots like this one.. [Photo: National Museum of Canada.]

As the lumber industry faded, the sea came to take its essential place in the economy of the town. Whereas since the beginning the sea had been the means of transportation for people and products, now fishing became the focus. An early chapter in commercial fisheries in Gouldsboro involved whaling. Based in Prospect Harbor, it was called "shore whaling." Try-works were built on the shore by Stephen Clark and Levi Hillier, who had come from Rochester, Massachusetts. June to September was whale season, when the animals followed the menhaden to shore. A whale when killed was towed to the harbor flats where it was cut up. The peak of that fishery was about 1840 and yielded six or seven whales a season. Ten was the largest recorded number, and each whale yielded twenty five to thirty barrels of oil. By about 1860 the whale fishery was dead in Gouldsboro.

Before the Civil War, hake fishing was pre-eminent. Frenchman's Bay often had as many as one hundred vessels, but once the hake left the bay roughly at the end of the Civil War that fishery declined. Menhaden were fished from about 1855 to about 1870. They were the bait that drew whales and hake into Frenchman's Bay, and they were a rich source of fish oil. During the same period in mid-century mackerel were sought in the Gulf of Saint Lawrence, where four or five vessels each year sailed. Though fishing for cod had been an essential part of New England economy from the seventeenth century, following the Civil War in Gouldsboro and other Maine towns,

109

there came a thrust to the Grand Banks of Newfoundland where rich fishing grounds opened possibilities of great harvests.

One example is the voyage of *Robert Rantoul, Jr.* Built in 1839 in Essex, Massachusetts, she was an eighty ton schooner with six foot draft. Her owner was Thomas Arey in Gouldsboro. In 1862 she made a fishing voyage to the Grand Banks. The owner was to receive one quarter of the profits, the shoremen curing the fish received one sixteenth share and the rest of the catch was divided among the fishermen, including the master of the vessel, in proportion to the fish each caught.

The master was Thomas R. Hammond, aged twenty seven. The crew, all residents of Gouldsboro, included seven fishermen. The oldest member was Nathan Shaw Hammond, aged fifty one, the captain's father; Ambrose Bourget, aged thirty seven, a French Canadian and the only member of the crew unable to sign his name; Augustus Benjamin Newman, aged thirty two; David Moore, aged twenty eight; Farnsworth Newman, aged twenty five; Nahum Jordan Joy, aged twenty four (on what proved to be his final voyage, dying three weeks later in the great diphtheria epidemic ravaging the port of Winter Harbor; and the youngest member of the crew, Edward J. Hammond, the master's brother, aged 12. The *Robert Rantoul, Jr.* set sail on 15

As the fishery for hake and cod shifted to larger ports after the 1860s, Gouldsboro fishermen turned to lobster fishing, providing product for the first canning factories in town. In time these same canneries turned instead to packaging herring to make canned sardines, providing work for crews like this one at the Holt factory in South Gouldsboro.
[Photo: Gouldsboro Historical Society.]

July 1862 on a voyage lasting four months and five days. The ship's journal noted on 20 November: "to Day returned to Gouldsboro and landed three hundred quintals [cured] fish." A quintal weighed 112 pounds, for a total catch of 33,600 pounds, or fifteen tons of fish.

Gouldsboro's fishing industry gradually morphed into today's more familiar lobster catch. In 1863 and 1870, the Portland Canning Company opened two plants in Gouldsboro to process small lobsters, the larger ones being sold to smacks from Portland and Boston. These companies operated four to five months a year, employing between them thirty men and twenty nine women, and produced in 1870 a total of 340,000 cans of lobster meat. Even as the canning industry shifted from lobsters to sardines after 1880, the number of lobster fishermen in that year rose to seventy eight fishermen, each with an average of sixty lobster pots or traps.

Vessels built locally contributed to the increasingly diversified economic underpinnings of Gouldsboro, but the economy in the nineteenth century included as well a broadened cargo trade. In the earliest days, the *Diana* and other ships had carried the lumber and wood products that were the foundation of the basic economy in expanded transport and wide ranging destinations. Custom House records reveal twenty five vessels built in Gouldsboro ship yards. Captain Jesse Perry (1804-1894) is a prime example of the scope of the Gouldsboro cargo trade.. Born in Gouldsboro, Perry followed the sea from age fourteen till age eighty. He was captured by Confederates in the Civil War when he skippered the brig *Whitaker.* At his death in West Bay, he left shares in seven vessels and accounts in four Boston banks.

The brig *Sullivan*, built in the Emery shipyard in West Bay, sailed for seventeen years. On her maiden voyage she carried hay from Portland to Savannah, where cotton was loaded for a voyage to Liverpool to supply the great cotton mills of Lancashire. Afterwards Emery used the *Sullivan* in the West Indies and South American trade. Later she was sold to New Bedford where her first voyage was to the west coast of Africa and brought home a load of whale oil and whale bone. During her second voyage from New Bedford, the seaworthy old Gouldsboro-built vessel was lost near the Cape Verde Islands. In ship ledgers from 1849 to 1863, Captain Perry recorded voyages of five vessels: the brigs *Noble, Whitaker,* and *Umpire*, and schooners *Gulnare* and *H. D. Leighton.* Mostly hauling coal, he sailed in those years to New Haven, New York, Boston, Philadelphia, Wilmington, North Carolina, Richmond and Alexandria in Virginia, Charleston, South Carolina, Satilla River, Georgia, Cuba, Bristol, Newport and

Providence in Rhode Island, Calais and Eastport in Maine, Portsmouth, New Hampshire, Tisbury in Martha's Vineyard, Salem and Dighton in Massachusetts, Pictou, Nova Scotia Jacksonville and Mayport in Florida, Martinique and Haiti, Puerto Rico, Washington, D.C., St Mary's and Somerset in Maryland, and to Jamaica.

Gouldsboro brigs and schooners were prominent in the shipping trade, carrying goods including coal to various ports worldwide, often at great cost when ships and crews were wrecked. [Gouldsboro Historical Society.]

This way of life was filled with danger. A case in point is the schooner *O. H. Perry.* Built in 1846, she was a vessel of 111 tons, with a value of $3000. In the winter of 1850 she was making a voyage from Bristol, Pennsylvania to Salem, Massachusetts loaded with 155 tons of coal. On Christmas Eve she was making her way near Martha's Vineyard through a heavy winter gale from the northwest. That morning citizens of the Vineyard saw the *O. H. Perry* stricken on rocks about five yards from shore. In that terrible night the sailors had cut away her masts and attempted to get a line ashore by a floating spar. The onlookers heard the cries for help coming from the crew, but in the turbulent seas the waves were monstrous. "One after another was seen to be washed from the vessel by the raging sea," the ledger recorded. By noon all were dead, eerily reminiscent of the *Diana* disaster nearly a century before. Next day, Christmas Day, the five bodies of the crew were washed ashore. They were Captain Charles E. Bunker, aged forty eight; Charles E. Spurling, aged twenty five; William A. Jones, aged twenty six, William T. Joy, aged thirty one, and William B. Sargent, youngest member of the crew, aged eighteen. Their bodies were buried in No Man's Land, a small uninhabited island three miles off the coast of the Vineyard. In the following spring, the bodies were exhumed and brought home to Gouldsboro where they were reburied near their homes in West Bay.

By 1870 four other industries had been added to the economic mix in Gouldsboro. Brothers James and Peter Hill had a tannery, water powered for a bark mill and splitting machine. Operating for eight or nine months in the year, they produced leather from cow and ox hides and calf skins. Only the owners worked in the tannery. William Wood had invested $500 in a fish weir and netting business. Employing three men, the business ran five months in the year. They used fish, salt, wooden casks and boxes and produced fish oil, fish chum (fish bone and blood processed into fish bait) and smoked herring. William Eaton's cabinet shop, with his employee Ephraim Wales Taft, used a jig saw, a lathe and a boring machine mobilized by water power. They produced furniture which generated $300 annually for wages, and the shop operated all year long. William Guptill's spool business also used waterpower for the circular saw. Two men were employed for whom $200 in wages were paid. The business operated four months of the year and used 150 cords of wood annually. In all these industries, wood was still a basic element, as it had in the beginning of Gouldsboro's life.

Agriculture was a basic way of life, providing much of the food for the town. In 1850 there were eighty two homesteads farming in the town, increased to ninety eight twenty years later. All of the farms had cows, made butter and grew Irish potatoes. Hay for feeding the livestock was cut on all the farms. As time passed, the power of oxen was gradually giving way to horses. In 1850 89% had oxen and 24% had horses, but by 1870 on 63% still used oxen and 35% had horses. Sheep raising also was declining. In 1850 sheep were raised in 85% of the farms with an average of 13 sheep per flock, but by 1870 only 72% had sheep with an average of nine per flock. In 1870 pigs were grown by 81% of the farmers, which was a higher percent than the 68% in 1850. Less land was "improved" (cleared and cultivated) at an average of 23 acres per farm, making 19% of the town in 1870, as opposed to an average of 40 acres per farm and 33% of the town in 1850.

Times were changing, as was the economy. In mid-century, under the potent influence of the artists who visited and painted Mount Desert Island-- Thomas Cole, Frederic Church, and Fitz Henry Lane- - summer colonies began. In spring of 1889 a corporation called Gouldsboro Land Improvement Company had an initial organizational

meeting in New York City. Five thousand acres of land were assembled on Grindstone Point in Gouldsboro at what was then called "the port of Winter Harbor," one of the Gouldsboro villages. The first lots, one acre each, were sold at a cost of $50.00.

A new day was beginning in Maine. The economy would turn more and more from total dependence on land and sea to tourism and summer trade. The old industries of fishing, canning, building, and farming continued to hold on, but a new economic strain was being added, based on Maine's beauty as a primary resource. The tourist and summer colony industry would go far beyond Gouldsboro to involve much of the state. The development of Grindstone Point would finally enable, in 1895, the legal separation of Winter Harbor from the old town of Gouldsboro, and raise it into an independent town.

With the ending of the nineteenth century, the independent status of Winter Harbor village as a new township in the State of Maine and the coming of the "rusticators", the old way of life would inevitably come to an end. No one grasped the massive changes, and expressed them more succinctly and evocatively, than Sarah Orne Jewett (1849-1909), the Maine author, in this excerpt from her 1896 sketches, *The Country of the Pointed Firs.*

> It was the time of late summer . . . all the light seemed to come through the green leaves . . . the clear high sky seemed to lift quickly . . . . There was no autumnal mist on the coast, nor any August fog; instead of these, the sea, the sky, all the long shore line, and the inland hills, with every bush of bay and every fir-top, gained a deeper color and a sharper clearness. There was something shining

in the air, and a kind of lustre on the water and the pasture grass, -- a northern look that, except at this moment of the year, one must go far to seek. The sunshine of a northern summer was coming to its lovely end . . . . The little town, with the tall masts of its disabled schooners in the inner bay, stood high above the flat sea for a few minutes, then it sank back into the uniformity of the coast and became indistinguishable from the other towns that looked as if they were crumbled on the furzy-green stoniness of the shore . . . . Presently the wind began to blow, and we struck out seaward to double the long sheltering headland of the cape, and when I looked back again, the islands and the headland had run together, and Dunnet Landing and all its coasts were lost to sight.

Sources

*Gilbert White *Journals.*
*Boston *Gazette,* January 1772.
*T. S. Eliot, *The Complete Poems and Plays.*
*Registers of Mortehoe Parish, Devon, Diocese of Exeter.
*Lloyd's *List*, 1770-1771.
*Deeds of Lincoln and Hancock Counties, Maine.
*Jesse Perry Account Book in author's possession.
*Perry Family Bible Record in author's possession.
*Probate of Jesse Perry estate in Hancock County.
William Bingham's Maine Lands, Frederick S. Allis, (ed.).
*Ephraim Wales Taft, ALS letter in author's possession.
*Federal Population, Agricultural and Industrial Censuses 1850, 1870.
*Waldo *Patriot*, 17 August 1838.
Eastern Star (Machias, Maine) in *Gazette*, Salem, MA, 15 July 1825.
Geographical Review of the Fisheries in Miscellaneous Documents of the Senate of the United States, 1881-1882.
*National Archives, Fishing and Shipping Agreements, State of Maine.
*Maine State Valuations of Vessels Owned in Gouldsboro.
*Tombstone inscription in West Bay Cemetery, Gouldsboro.
*Massachusetts Tax List 1798, New England Historic Genealogical Society.
Documentary History of the State of Maine, Volume 14.
*"Geographical Review of the Fisheries" in *The Miscellaneous Documents of the Senate of the United States* 1881-'82.

Chapter *10*

A GOULDSBORO TRAGEDY "MOST SACRILEGIOUS MURDER"

Gouldsboro's 1938 Town Constable, Irving Hinckley, the first to discover Frank Crowhurst's murdered body.

(Daring Detective [magazine], v.9 n.54.)

This vivid tale, describing what was probably Gouldsboro's most notorious murder case, was delivered by Rev. Joy at the Old Town House Museum in August of 2013. This talk reflects Joy's devotion to the town and village life that is his own heritage, as well as his appreciation of how the community in the early 20th Century was continuing to absorb people from elsewhere, adding to the rich historical texture of Gouldsboro.

§

Confusion now hath made his masterpiece!
Most sacrilegious murder hath broke ope
The Lord's anointed temple, and stole thence
The life o' the building."
Macbeth II, 3

Summer 1938. In Europe clouds were gathering. The nations were grumbling toward war. The Franco government in Spain was recognized by Britain and France. Hitler's Anschluss of Austria increased not only the territory of the Third Reich but edged the world closer toward conflict. In Germany itself the Flossenburg concentration camp was opened. Kristallnacht with massive destruction of Jewish shops and synagogues in Germany was a harbinger of still more terrible things to come.

In America the economy, while recovering and gaining strength, was still wobbly from the Depression. The New Deal had been introduced by President Franklin Roosevelt, but his popularity was beginning to wane. Congress passed a minimum wage law guaranteeing workers twenty five cents per hour with a maximum of forty four hours in the working week, at the seventy fifth anniversary of the Battle of Gettysburg, President Roosevelt dedicated the Eternal Light Peace Memorial, and lit the eternal flame. In the month of September New England was struck by a hurricane with 183 mile per hour winds. Cooperstown, New York, rejoiced in the opening of the Baseball Hall of Fame. On a lighter note, Superman first appeared in comics, and instant coffee was invented. In January, the play *Our Town* by Thornton Wilder·· depicting a New Hampshire village not unlike Gouldsboro·· was premiered in New York and received the Pulitzer Prize. Summer 1938 saw the Munich sellout agreement with

Hitler, called by diplomat Madeleine Albright "the long days of that unlovely summer."

Adolph Hitler was the scourge of Germany and the talk of the world, but in Gouldsboro, Maine, all was peace. On Monday, 25th July, sunrise happened at 5.11. At 8 o'clock, bright sunshine by 8 o'clock was welcome after a day and night of heavy rain and thick fog tolling in from the sea out of Jones's Cove.

Irving Hinckley, aged sixty nine, local farmer and constable of Gouldsboro, was heading early to Ellsworth and needed gas. His tank was on empty. He went to Frank Crowhurst's tavern on Route One just above West Gouldsboro village, where beer and sandwiches and Hancock County ice cream were sold, as well as gas. The brand was Mobil and it cost $.20 per gallon. With Hinckley in the car were his wife Ida, aged fifty four, a worker in the sardine factory, and their granddaughter Ruth M. Grindle, aged six. Oddly, the window shades were still drawn at the tavern. Constable Hinckley blew the horn but there was no movement. Finding the door unlocked, he went inside and called out, "Frank, I want some gas."

In front of the tavern building was the gas tank. Inside was a large lunch room and beer parlor with a counter and stools, a telephone booth and small store with basic supplies. An "immaculate kitchen"

Frank Crowhurst's body where he fell behind the counter was much photographed by news sources. [Official Detective [magazine], v. vii n.2.]

was directly behind the counter, and a small personal apartment, residence of Frank Crowhurst, in the rear.

Heading toward the apartment through the dim room, Hinckley stumbled on Crowhurst's body. He raised the shades and saw at once that the man was dead, the body jammed against the door of the telephone booth. He hurried out to this wife Ida. "Go across the street to the town hall and telephone Deputy Sheriff Blance in Winter Harbor and tell him to get here as quickly as possible." (The town hall back then was today's Old Town House.) Blance arrived at 8:45 and telephoned Sheriff Hodgkins in Ellsworth, where the body was taken to Hurley Hospital for autopsy by Dr Knowlton. The verdict was "multiple comminuted fractures of the skull," which meant murder.

So who was this murdered man Frank Crowhurst, rather an exotic in West Gouldsboro, "one of the most colorful characters ever to adopt our state?" He was born in Brighton, Sussex, on the south English coast, at 2 St Peter's Street on 3 October 1869, one of several children of Albert Crowhurst, "fly driver." The fly was a fast light covered two wheel carriage invented in Brighton in 1816. It was drawn in the beginning by men, like a Chinese litter, then by horse. It could be hired like a cab. His mother Emma was a Londoner, a dressmaker.

In 1891, at the age of twenty two, Frank Crowhurst worked as a domestic waiter for Brighton wine merchant John K. Stead. On 7 February 1892 he sailed from Liverpool on the steamship Teutonic, White Star Line. She was the first armed merchant cruiser, at that time a new ship only three years old. The arrival date was 11 February after four days passage to Ellis Island in New York. His quarters were forward in the ship and he carried a single piece of luggage, doubtless a steamer trunk. The emigration was completed when, six years later on 2 September 1898 he declared his intention to become an American citizen with the "intention to renounce forever all allegiance and fidelity to Victoria, Queen of the United Kingdom of Great Britain and Ireland and Empress of India, of whom I am a subject." His naturalization was completed on 4 November 1914 when he was living as a butler in domestic service in the household at 905 Ridge Avenue, Pittsburg, Pennsylvania. His appearance, self-described in a later passport application, was 5'8 in height, mouth small, forehead high, eyes brown, hair grayish, complexion ruddy and face round.

Perhaps the most formative connection of his life was as valet and butler to Robert Hall McCormick, Jr, grandson of Cyrus McCormick, inventor of the mechanical reaper. Robert McCormick, born in Virginia in 1847, was director of the American Harvester Company. A resident of Chicago, his summer home, Mizzentop, was at

119

Bar Harbor. Later the home burned in the great fire of 1947, its foundations still visible under the Bluenose Inn. Among his many interests were horses, yachting, and art. He owned one of the finest collections of British master paintings in the United States. For many seasons, Frank Crowhurst his valet had sailed with him on the 120 foot yacht *Rapidan* to far places in the world. Mementos of these travels decorated the tavern lunchroom in Gouldsboro, a "unique interior with its curious treasures, [including bright Indian blankets] collected from all over the world." McCormick died in March 1917 in Augusta, Georgia.

Later, in the same year his employer's died, Crowhurst married McCormick's cook on 24 October in Bar Harbor. Two years older than her groom, Christine Henderson Crowhurst was born in the village of Clouden at Holywood, Dumfriesshire, Scotland. Her father Robert Henderson was a miller, her mother Margaret a cook. Christine went into service at an early age, training as "kitchen maid" at Hackwood House at Hexham, Northumberland, England, estate of wealthy banker John Oswald Head, whose only son Reginald would be killed at Gallipoli in 1915. The way of life "in service" to lordly patrons was laid early for both the Crowhursts.

As the beginning of a new life in their marriage, and building on their experience and training, the couple used their joint savings to invest in the four story forty-room Wayside Inn Hotel in West Gouldsboro. On 1 November 1917, with a mortgage for $2000, they bought from Samuel G. Wood two lots of land and the Inn building that had been erected about 1800 by Abijah Jones. The mortgage was discharged in 1920. "Under their management, it became famous along the New England coast for its excellent cuisine and comfortable accommodations." Increasing prosperity enabled the Crowhursts to accomplish several other real estate transactions in West Gouldsboro, including a camp lot on the shore of nearby Jones's Pond, for a total of some 150 acres.

Christine Crowhurst underwent three strokes, complicated by diabetes. She died in January 1933, aged sixty five, and was buried in Lakeview Cemetery where they had bought a quarter of Lot 13. Frank Crowhurst carried on the hotel alone until January 1936, when the building caught fire from a faulty chimney and burned flat. There was no insurance. He then rebuilt a small lunch room and gas station, his tavern just up the hill from the ruins of the Wayside Hotel.

In May 1938, the new building completed, Crowhurst applied for a license "to sell malt liquors at his restaurant in West Gouldsboro." In that same month he entered upon his final real estate transaction when he sold to Frank P. Noyes the thirty one acres he had bought in 1917. So the scene was laid for summer 1938, the murder and its motive.

Crowhurst had been owner of the original Wayside Inn, a venerable hostelry in West Gouldsboro before it burned. Thereafter he continued to serve customers in his tavern at the intersection just uphill from the old inn. (Gouldsboro Historical Society photo.)

The discovery of Frank Crowhurst's body revealed that the back and top of his head had been struck with what appeared to be a peen hammer or heavy wrench, most of the blows administered after he had fallen to the floor. The most pitiful detail reported was that "in his right hand he clutched fifty or sixty hairs from his own head," meaning that he instinctively reached up as the first blow fell on the crown of his head. It was at first thought that the motive was robbery, but money was discovered in his pocket, in the cash register, in his wallet, under paper in the top bureau drawer, and in a chest in his bedroom. The violence of the attack indicated passion rather than greed.

Crowhurst's Lake View Tavern became a magnet for spectators as news spread of the murder. [Official Detective [magazine], v. vii n.2.]

The process of search and discovery began. It was revealed that the last sale of gas at the front pump, 2 7/10 gallons costing 54 cents, was made at seven o'clock on the previous night. A witness saw him last alive at 8:30 that night speaking to men in a green sedan bearing Rhode Island license plates. By 9:30 the establishment was in darkness. In his bedroom on the night table was found a loaded revolver, and it was determined that he was trying to telephone for help, or reach his gun, when he was struck on top of the head from behind and fell. So began the investigation.

Interviews included Milford Coombs of Winter Harbor, aged forty, who on June 1st had begun working for Crowhurst serving beer and lunches, and pumping gas. During his interview Coombs mentioned Ada Young who had also been working for Crowhurst, getting ready for the summer rush. She had been employed by Crowhurst on and off since she was 14. Coombs also mentioned problems with a man who was Ada's fiancé. In this way they were led to Howard Merry, the man who would be arrested, tried and convicted for Frank Crowhurst's murder. So who was he?

Merry was a man far different from Frank Crowhurst. Son of Canadian parents, he was born in 1910 in Kingston, Massachusetts.

His father was a teamster and a laborer in an iron foundry. Having finished the ninth grade, he began working on a cousin's dairy farm in Duxbury, Massachusetts. Married in 1932, he was divorced only two years later. In 1935, he was tried in Massachusetts for attempting to hire a killer for the husband of a woman he was interested in, and in that same year he moved to Maine, where he lived with his sister Olive and her husband Maynard Jellison on Georges Pond Road in Franklin. Merry worked first at Triangle Garage in Ellsworth, then in 1936 for William Emery in his auto body shop. He sported as his vehicle a 1931 model four passenger Essex coupe, black with yellow wheels.

The accused murderer, Howard Merry. [Daring Detective [magazine], v.9 n.54.]

His description in 1938 paints a picture of the man. He was twenty eight, a "compactly built man," bushy browed with thinning hair, well-mannered but appearing to be easily upset emotionally. His sister Olive later said she "never asked him about his plans as he had such a quick temper and grew angry when questioned about his movements."

In November 1937, eight months before Frank Crowhurst was murdered, he began to date Ada Young. He was reported to have been fascinated by her, and very possessive. In early 1938 Merry was arrested for shooting deer out of season. After "pestering Ada for the past four months," he gave Ada an engagement ring. He insisted strongly that she leave Crowhurst's employ, but she was unwilling. She was paid $2 to $5 dollars a day. She later testified she was not required to wear a uniform to work because "he [as a former butler and valet who had been trained in service] told me I was not a servant." Appreciating this, she also testified, "I thought as much of him as I do of my own father," and Milford Coombs reported that Frank Crowhurst, childless widower, treated Ada Young "as he would a daughter of his own."

Merry was unrelenting is his pursuit of this obviously ambivalent woman who clearly knew nothing of his marital and romantic past. He "haunted the station practically every night," parking his car to obstruct customers for the tavern, shined his car lights through the windows to annoy customers inside, and would even go inside and glare at any customers with whom Ada spoke. Frank Crowhurst finally told Ada she would have to give up her job for Merry.

Ada Young, the object of Merry's unwanted attentions. (Official Detective [magazine], v. vii n.2.)

In response Ada, in an awkward position, quit the tavern on 5 July and began working at a new job in Ellsworth. The climax came on Saturday 23 July. Ada and Merry went to a dance in Waltham. She danced with another young man. Merry was jealous. He and Ada fought; she returned her five day old engagement ring and told him that on Monday she was going to leave her job in Ellsworth, call Frank Crowhurst and return to his employment.

Police attention now turned fully to Howard Merry. The highlights of the investigation appeared at his trial. Merry was arrested on 24 August and arraigned in Ellsworth on 1 September, indicted by the Grand Jury.

Much of Ellsworth had been destroyed in a great fire in 1933. The courthouse had been rebuilt, and in that new building the trial of Howard Merry opened on 1 October. The jury was sequestered in isolation in a special dining room of the Hancock House at the foot of Bridge Hill. Thirty three witnesses appeared for the state, "an avalanche of testimony," and a throng of onlookers. Merry's clothing, with areas of bloodstain cut out, was a major exhibit. "The effect was sieve-like but not gruesome." Through the trial Merry was reported "without a trace of emotion, utterly impassive." It was very different from earlier behavior

It was a confusing case but it is possible to distill the trial and the display of evidence. First, there was the intermittent engagement to Ada Young and his "angry irritation" at her employment by Crowhurst. Second was Merry's distinctive car was seen on Sunday night parked by Crowhurst's service station between 8:15 and 8:30. Third, Merry had a false alibi. He said he had left Ada Young's house by 8:15 on Sunday night, drove to North Sullivan to get a friend, Norman Hicks, to go with him to a movie in Ellsworth: "Yellow Jack," starring Robert Montgomery and Virginia Bruce. It was playing at the new Grand Theater which had only just opened on 14 July and "offers the public of this vicinity the best in modern entertainment and comfort." He said, however, that the Hicks house was dark; he started alone for Ellsworth, changed his mind and turned at Franklin Road and went home to his sister's where he was living. He stated that he had arrived at 9:30 to find that his sister was entertaining company. He changed his clothes and came downstairs to do dishes. Norman Hicks, however, testified in rebuttal that the lights at his house, front and back, were lit at 8:15 and burned until 10. This destroyed Merry's alibi for the time of the murder. Fourth, Merry claimed he was wearing a blue serge suit on Sunday night. It was proved that he was indeed wearing a blue coat but beige slacks, "which we found rolled up in a trunk in his room, newly washed, but with clear evidence of blood stains." There was of course no testing then for DNA, but it was proved to be human blood. Blood was found also on the blue coat which he claimed came from a nosebleed.

The jury deliberated on 6 October from 4:30 until 8. They found him guilty of the murder of Frank Crowhurst, described by the medical examiner Dr. Charles Knowlton as "a peculiarly revolting crime." An appeal was denied, and on 23 September 1939 he began a sentence of life imprisonment in the state penitentiary at Thomaston where, in 1940, he was confined in cell 7097.

What was the aftermath of the murder and trial? On 24 November 1939 two lots in Gouldsboro, late the property of Frank Crowhurst, were sold to John H. and Elizabeth R. Fox of Yonkers, Westchester County, New York. The sellers were the remaining living siblings of Frank Crowhurst. They were Thomas Charles Crowhurst, widower, of 42 St Paul Street in Brighton, Sussex; Charlotte Crowhurst Unwins, widow, of 12 Church Road, Portslade by Sea, Sussex; and Ellen Crowhurst Page and William T. E. Page, her husband, of 11 Wilfred Road, Hove, Sussex, "heirs at law and next of kin." The transaction of sale was accomplished at the Consulate General and Embassy of the United States at London in Mayfair.

Howard Merry sought and obtained commutation of his life sentence from Horace Hildreth, governor of Maine, on 17 November 1948. Merry was released in 1949 and he died 17 January 1976 at Plymouth, Massachusetts.

Frank Crowhurst enjoyed a stellar reputation in the town he had adopted as home. In the Wayside Hotel and later in the tavern, he was a "cheerful and genial proprietor;" his "personality drew many customers" who "flocked from every place." Milford Coombs his employee said "He was one of the nicest men I ever knew." In West Gouldsboro it was said the held "a prominent and respected niche in local society." Ada Young "confirmed stories of his kindliness and readiness to help anyone down on his luck," supported by a local person who said "everybody here in Gouldsboro always had a good word for him. He wasn't much at talking but always ready to give everybody a hand."

At the 1938 site of Crowhurst's Lake View Tavern, the entire highway has been rebuilt, with a substantially rebuilt structure on the property at the Clinic Road intersection shown here. This site is just across Route One from the Old Town House, where Rev. Joy in his talk described the once notorious events surrounding the murder.

It was a Gouldsboro tragedy. "Confusion now hath made his masterpiece! Most sacrilegious murder hath broke ope the Lord's anointed temple and stole the life o' the building." The fly driver's son had worked hard. He had left his home and moved to an adopted country. He had had an interesting and varied life. He had accomplished much after, at the age of twenty two, he passed the Statue of Liberty, lifting her lamp beside the golden door. It is hard not to consider his story a modern tragedy. The long journey came to an abrupt, violent and tragic ending, and the golden door slammed closed. He and Christine Henderson are quiet under a stone in Lakeview Cemetery.

He enjoyed a fine reputation among those with whom he lived and worked, causing one to remember the words of the Bible: "The memory of the just is blessed." But that abrupt and terrible end can call to mind another sobering reflection from the Bible, words read when his parents were buried with the Church of England liturgy in the Book of Common Prayer: "The days of our age are threescore years and ten, and though men be so strong that they come to fourscore years, yet is their strength then but labor and sorrow, so soon passeth it away and we are gone."

Sources

* "Maine's Tavern Mystery and the Silent Witness," *Daring Detective* [magazine], v.9 n.54 (1938), pp 26-29 & 68.
* "The Girl Who Wouldn't Say 'No' ," *Official Detective* [magazine], v. vii n.2 (1938), pp 19-21 & 45.
* *Ellsworth American* (27 July and 31 August 1938) and *Bangor Daily News* (5 October 1938).
* British censuses of 1861, 1881 and 1891 in England and Scotland for Frank and Christine (Henderson) Crowhurst.
*Hancock County Deeds and Probate; Vital Records of Maine;
*Records if Passengers in Port of Entry for New York; Records of Naturalization; Records of Passport Applications; US Censuses 1920 and 1930.
*For Howard Merry: Vital Records of Massachusetts; US Censuses 1920, 1930 and 1940; Social Security Records of Deaths.
*Portland Press Herald (17 November 1948) and State of Maine, Commutation of Sentence 17 November 1948.

Appendix A

Gouldsboro's Contentious Path to Statehood

William King of Bath, Maine, elected to the Massachusetts Legislature at a critical point in 1816, managed to negotiate an end to the interstate tariff system, thus freeing Maine commerce to trade nationwide without its former dependence on Massachusetts. This new freedom opened the way to independent statehood in 1819 and 1820, eventually with support from Gouldsboro. King became Maine's first Governor. [Gilbert Stuart portrait 1806, Maine Governor's Office]

This editorial essay on the 1812 war and progress toward statehood is based on a talk by Allen Workman at the Gouldsboro Historical Society, June 6, 2016.

§

Along with the rest of Maine, the downeast region grew between 1785 and 1820 from a thinly populated region into a burgeoning coastal community with a restless but developing up-country hinterland. Starting as a remote part of Massachusetts in a new nation, the region that included Gouldsboro slowly grew and survived wartime humiliation to finally gain a new sense of self-confidence and then independence as part of a new state. After the Revolution the region had emerged as a shattered outpost region dominated by colonial merchant proprietors, completely dependent on ties to Boston to feed and clothe itself, and with an ill-defined sense of where it belonged in the New England region and the new nation. The downeast townships rose up slowly, began questioning their old dependency, and were gradually forced into an ambivalent and even negative relationship to the nation, before they could rebound from the 1812 war to develop self-confidence and sustainable resources for a strong role in the economy of the northeast.

By 1800 the downeast region had gained a big influx of settlers since the end of the 1780s, with newly developed town centers at Ellsworth, Bangor, Blue Hill, and Eastport gaining 60-100% in population. The young settlements downeast had been authorized to govern themselves as towns for barely a decade, newly given authority to tax, organize, and attempt to enforce land titles. These earliest townsmen had just begun to reach a tenuous sense of being part of American nationhood. They were not quite free from an earlier colonial mentality which expected wealthy land proprietors to take care of broader political concerns, while giving a fair shake to smaller homesteaders. This pattern is a leading theme for a well-respected study of this era—*Liberty Men and Great Proprietors* by historian Alan Taylor. He emphasized how most settlers, preoccupied with securing their immediate subsistence and self-conscious about their limited education, felt they had no business participating in politics beyond the local. Policy decisions and trade connections were to be decided by the large landowning proprietors with their connections to Boston.

In Gouldsboro Nathan Jones, as an early proprietor, had been taking on regional and commercial affairs as far as they affected his family's extensive territory. In 1795 he was joined by a much larger operator, the Bingham proprietorship and its agent, General David Cobb, tasked with administering land sales in a vast territory as well as for more than half of Gouldsboro's territory. Cobb's goal, to regularize and even to civilize the Town's rough-hewn settlers, was only partially successful, but he brought stability to government, infrastructure, and especially to land tenure. He expressed his ambitions for this rough-hewn town in no uncertain terms, in letters to Bingham in England:

"I have been preaching the principles of civilization to the people.... explaining the rights of property to them.... In a short time the present passion for plunder will cease and agricultural industry succeed." (David Cobb to William Bingham, December, 1796)

Cobb commissioned a survey of the unsold Gouldsboro land, laying it out into well-defined lots priced from a dollar an acre for woods to three or four dollars for harbor plots. By 1800 Cobb and John Black, together with Nathan Jones and his associates, now closely related by marriage, were the biggest landowners· in town along with the Bingham proprietors. For the next twenty years these owners dominated the town's government and its role in Massachusetts state politics, Cobb serving prominently with distinction in many state offices, religiously adhering to the Federalist party program. Gouldsboro townsmen came to rely heavily on their powerful patron to look after their interests. The 1810 town population of 480 had 92 householders—mostly considered "freeholders" and therefore voters. Of these, a majority core of 30- 40 of those voters consistently supported their patron's Federalist candidates. While only 22% of householders tended to vote for U.S. congressman, the Federalists turned out a high of 62% of the town's householders in the 1812 presidential race to vote almost unanimously against the hated embargo Democrats, Thomas Jefferson and James Madison. Town offices were held by less than a dozen freeholders, mostly from West Bay and West Gouldsboro, though a few from the gradually growing Prospect and Winter Harbor areas began to participate---a sign that the fishing industry was picking up

During this era, before the growth of free interstate commerce, Maine benefited from a unique "Coastwise Trade" Federal law that was to play a distinctive role in its future history. Merchants in each state were required to pay a duty on all trade with other states—**excepting trade with the states immediately bordering it.** Maine, as part of Massachusetts, was therefore considered contiguous to every coastal state in the northeast including New York, thus allowing free trade for its fish and lumber, and sustaining its lifeline of imports from the prosperous coastline to the south. And of course Gouldsboro continued its longstanding dependence on commerce with Boston and beyond to reach critical markets for timber and fish and gain vital imports for the still remote town. Thus the convenience of contiguous borders would continue to keep Maine tied to Massachusetts and its trade. With this benefit the commercial fishery downeast began to grow exponentially. Somewhat larger vessels capable of working the offshore banks also benefited from new U.S. fishing bounty laws, the first of several intended to encourage the industry and maritime capabilities. Because of these benefits, coastal towns like Gouldsboro voted consistently against early proposals of separation from Massachusetts and in favor of Federalist-supported pro-maritime measures. Opposing the coastal districts, the upland regions' small farmers tended to favor the defiant views of agrarian Jeffersonian Democrats.

These rather entrenched political attitudes were disrupted as the Napoleonic wars of the early 1800s piled up problems for American merchants' booming neutral trade, resulting in Jefferson's hated Embargo on shipping to foreign ports in 1807. Inevitably the coastal communities

Massachusetts contiguous states in 1818

--OPEN for DUTY-FREE TRADE

Under the early American system of tariff duty between states-- except those immediately contiguous-- Maine had a big trade advantage as part of Massachusetts. The bracketed area here—all of New England and New York --was open for duty-free trade—which would be lost if Maine were to become independent.

howled in indignation as their livelihoods dried up. Coastal Mainers openly resisted the efforts of U.S. Federal forces enforcing embargo restrictions from forts at Eastport, Machias, and Castine. In little more than a year the failed embargo measure was repealed, but tensions were mounting, and a new awareness of the region's broader role was developing.

General Cobb became increasingly embroiled in these political battles back in Boston, taking on more state offices (Lieutenant Governor, Governor's Councilman) becoming more and more an absentee land manager as he spent time at the capital. He was loyally supported in Gouldsboro as defender of their vital trading interests— he had become "our man in Boston." As Cobb's assistant John Black began shifting his own operations to the growing town of Ellsworth, their place in managing Gouldsboro affairs was now filled by staunch traditional allies, Jones's neighbor Thomas Hill, Nathan Shaw, and Cobb's sons, but also some new landowners like Abijah Cole and Samuel Davis from more remote parts of town were serving as selectmen.

When President Madison and a hothead Congress stumbled into a declaration of war against Britain in June of 1812, Maine and especially the downeast were caught in the middle, unsure of what loyalties, if any, they owed to the national government. The coastal regions continued to reject any war measures that cut off their trade lifeline, including their commercial links to British-ruled Canadian Maritime provinces. Coastal towns were willing to raise local militias for home defense, appointing war opponents like Cobb and Black as militia officers. But at Eastport, townsmen resented the border contingent of troops from the Federal army, continuing to defy them while running a brisk and blatant contraband trade with Maritime Canadians who needed American supplies.

As the war opened, Gouldsboro's Town Meeting of August 3, 1812 adopted a resolution --- (possibly drafted by Thomas Hill or Nathan Shaw)-- that perfectly expressed a new sense of the town's role in national affairs. It was resolved "that we are firmly attached to the Federal Constitution; and believe that under an upright and faithful Administration of it, we might and still enjoy, prosperity and safety," but "that we will not voluntarily aid nor assist in the prosecution of an offensive War, which we believe to be neither just, necessary, nor expedient...." But as trade was drying up by the next April of 1813, another Gouldsboro vote noted that "in these times of poverty and distress ... people are almost driven to the brink for means of

132

supporting life." The war's slowdown of maritime commerce had taken a severe toll on the downeast's lifelines.

Because the governments of the New England states (though not necessarily the back country) were notoriously opposed to the war, the Royal Navy at first refrained from blockading the Northeast's coastwise trade. Unfortunately this did not save the coastal lifeline, as many mariners on both sides of the Canadian border decided to compensate for losing foreign trade by outfitting as privateer warships—unleashing legalized piracy and turmoil all over the Gulf of Maine. More than 190 New England privateers—mostly from west of the Penobscot-- captured over 200 vessels, while British warships and privateers did comparable damage. By July of 1813 the British Navy proceeded to cut off and capture all of Maine's fishing vessels, bringing this growing industry to a halt for some years.

On the Canadian side, the Provincial governments maintained an uneasy truce as well as a brisk contraband border trade, for the Maritime Provinces were still dependent on supplies from New England for most of their goods, including food. Meanwhile the British war against privateers was choking off shipping, just as widespread crop failures in the summer of 1813 depleted food supplies, and times grew desperate. Then the war situation overseas heated up as Napoleon surrendered unconditionally by April of 1814 and freed the British to concentrate on the American war. British raids intensified on the Maine coast in summer of 1814, bent on destroying shipping and commerce. Then the campaign against Maine took a more serious turn. The loyalists in the New Brunswick legislature petitioned the British Secretary of War to authorize a major force under General Sir John Sherbrooke, first to seize Eastport and then to occupy all of eastern Maine, since loyalists had long considered "the river Penobscot present[s] a 'natural boundary'" open to Canadian opportunities. On July 11 of 1814 a buildup of British land and sea forces assaulted and took Eastport without a fight—the beginning of the campaign that would "re-occupy" the entire downeast, again to become His Majesty's once-planned province of New Ireland.

Throughout the summer of 1814 marauding British vessels were raiding in coves and harbors, seeking to damage or confiscate local shipping and supplies. There is a tradition that General Cobb's house was fired upon with chain shot by a British raider, and that nearby stonework may have housed military supplies. Near today's Southwest Harbor, the British warship *Tenedos,* aiming to destroy ships across the water in Norwood Cove, sent in an armed barge that was fired upon by local resisters, killing three crewmen and forcing the raiders to retreat and depart.

About the same time, in a similar incident, a Yankee smuggling schooner *"Defiance"* was chased by the British brig *"Bruin,"* and when the Yankee sought safety in the shoal water of Pigeon Hill sound, it was pursued by another British landing barge. When the Yankee schooner fired a surprise broadside, killing three British sailors and capturing others, both sides called a truce and exchanged captives. It turned out that the captive Americans, guests of the Royal Navy on the brig, were none other than two of Gouldsboro's prominent Federalists‑ ‑ Ebenezer Cobb, the General's son, and William Shaw the proprietor's son (see Chapter Three). Whether these men had been caught in contraband shipping or in some other exchange, their presence aboard suggested close communication in the region between some in Gouldsboro and the British.

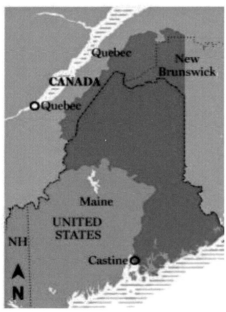

By the fall of 1814 all of Maine east of the Penobscot had fallen to the British, governed from Castine as a new Canadian province, as it had been during the Revolution under the name "New Ireland."

While British forces elsewhere were busy burning Washington and besieging Baltimore, they now mobilized forces for a planned occupation of the remaining downeast region, starting with Machias. By chance, however, their force of four warships and ten troop transports fell in with another British man-o-war pursuing the American frigate *Adams* up the Penobscot, so Sir John Sherbrooke decided instead to descend upon Castine. On September 1, 1814, the town and old fort were promptly abandoned by the 28 outgunned American Regulars there, and the British quickly captured the downriver region near Blue Hill and Orrington. They quickly scattered some Maine militia, among whom may have been a unit with three militiamen from Gouldsboro—Francis

Taft and the brothers John and William Bunker. Moving upriver, British forces faced American resistance at Hampden, where a brief battle was settled with a single charge of His Majesty's Regulars. The way was open for the capture of Bangor, which surrendered unconditionally and was subjected to considerable damage. On September 12 the British finished their occupation of the downeast, descending on Machias without resistance and securing a formal "civil capitulation" eventually signed by all the militia units in Washington County. They agreed to parole themselves not to resist and to "consider ourselves under the British government until further orders." Clearly these downeasters like most others were disgusted with the lack of support available from both Federal and State sources and were ready to take whatever was to come under a British regime. While the occupiers were destined to govern the region from Castine only until April the following year of 1815, none of the Mainers suspected this outcome at the time.

With the civil capitulations at Machias, His Majesty's empire was now nominally enlarged with a new Canadian province, one which had been set up earlier during the Revolution under the name of New Ireland. As most locals quickly adapted to the demands of the new regime, townsmen were required to swear nonresistance under two categories. Most desirable to the new regime was swearing an oath of allegiance to the Crown that allowed the full rights of a British subject, including authorization to conduct mercantile operations from Castine to St John and Halifax. A few merchants and shipowners chose this risky but profitable course, while most settled for an oath of neutrality. This type of offer from the Crown allowed retaining firearms for self-defense if sworn not to be used against the British. On September 13, the day of the Machias region's "civil capitulation," Gouldsboro townsmen formally voted to accept that offer.

However, Yankee and Canadian privateer actions at sea and British raids farther west created chaotic maritime conditions, completely shutting down most of the state's fishery. A contraband and smuggling trade was now shifted away from Eastport and centered in Castine and across the Penobscot throughout the winter of 1814-15. Local Yankees in this trade risked official penalties from the American side, but these were deeply resented and widely ignored because everybody was desperate for whatever supplies and food could be exchanged. In fact the British at Castine encouraged the contraband, and found they could be largely provisioned by helpful Maine smugglers. Meanwhile the Maine militia units west of the Penobscot were not able to mobilize much resistance to recover the lost territory. For one thing its officers were in discord, with some Federalists like Cobb and Black traditionally opposing the war and others like the Jeffersonian Democrat William King supporting it. When King sought

Massachusetts Governor Caleb Strong ignored Maine's wartime distress and actively courted British finances for Boston's advantage. Postwar resentment of this neglect for Maine helped fuel the drive for statehood. [Engraving by James Bannister for the American Bank Note Company - Restoration by Godot13.]

help for Maine, he found that the impoverished Federal government was helpless, and that Boston's legislature with Federalist Governor Caleb Strong were more than actively hostile to the war. In financial desperation Strong had already sought help from Bingham's and Baring's Bank for British loans, strictly to protect Boston. Pleas for help for Maine were thus ignored, and roundly rejected by Governor Strong and the State legislature-- rejections that were bitterly resented and long remembered after the war.

Meanwhile in faraway Europe the British government, fearing the collapse of a key diplomatic conference and wearied of continued war expenses, suddenly decided on a quick settlement with American negotiators on Christmas Eve, 1814, leaving both sides with exactly the same territory as before the war. The news did not reach New York till February 11 along with news of Jackson's recent victory in New Orleans. The downeast did not learn until February 14, and Halifax not until the 19th. British troops evacuated Castine and Machias on April 25, 1815, but were still unwilling to give up Eastport, where their troops stayed until June of 1818 due to drawn-out negotiations on the status of the Canadian border.

Undoubtedly many in the downeast region and others in Maine and New England had been uncertain during this controversial war about where their allegiances should lie. Yet it's clear that even those most friendly to Britain never had any desire to rejoin His Majesty's empire.

For example, voters in Gouldsboro—*a full two weeks before* any official news of war's end or of possible British departure reached the region-- expressed a desire for local business as usual as they gathered January 30 to dutifully elect yet another Federalist to represent them in the Congress of the United States. In April those same voters even managed to re-elect their Federalist Governor, Caleb Strong, whose indifference to their occupation would soon become notorious. Likely news had not reached them of Strong's disdain for the occupied Mainers, or his dispatching a Castine man to explore how the British would react if New England states should secede from the Union. In time such craven dealings would provoke bitter resentments throughout Maine, as would continuing unrest in border towns at Eastport and Presque Isle. By 1815 the trials of war had forced downeasters to take some different views of their links to the region and nation. They had been shaken in their assumption that powerful patrons would take care of necessary connections to the wider world, though many had not yet processed how their old connections and dependencies had been altered by the war crisis.   Meanwhile as Mainers strove to recover from ravages of war and crop failure, a natural disaster struck farming throughout the nation. In 1816 —"the year without a summer"—volcanic dust choked off normal climate throughout the northern hemisphere, and in most of Maine the ground was still frozen in May and into June. At length a slow buildup of farming and food production resumed in the years before 1820, and by that time population increases and land use had developed some distinctive patterns.

Despite the war people had continued to move into the downeast. In the decade up to 1820 Hancock County grew by about a third. The same was true of Washington County, mostly in new towns, while Steuben gained over 40 percent in size before it split into new townships. Gouldsboro's growth by comparison was quite modest at a 16% population increase. A great deal of the land in older downeast towns had been cleared by the end of the decade, and much of the timber lands in settled areas had been replaced by fields or pasture, especially in towns westward from Frenchman Bay. But throughout the downeast and especially from Gouldsboro eastward, the biggest growth industry was another kind of enterprise.

Shipping and fishing had been devastated by the embargo and then disastrously cut off by British incursions, but at the same time Mainers became aware of the heightened worldwide demand that came from a generation of international warfare, brisk neutral shipping, and especially smuggling.   Downeast mariners were eager to take advantage of the nation's demand for fish, and though Maine's overall tonnage in fishing craft was near zero in 1815, by the early 1820s its

137

tonnage had boomed to reach almost 20% of that in the entire U.S. In these years a new Federal measure responded to the market for fish as well as to some Canadian restrictions, but especially to a perceived need for more mariners and a stronger Navy. A new subsidy was provided for fishing craft-- a Federal bounty payment to all fishermen for their time at sea. By 1819 the bounty was broadened to include smaller schooner craft—the vessels that became the mainstay of enterprise for the local families and neighborhood groups that drove the cod fishery from this time until well past the Civil War era. In Gouldsboro this development helped fuel a surge of growth in its harbor villages from South Gouldsboro to Winter and Prospect Harbors to Indian Harbor, bringing the area into a brisk convergence with the fisheries of the other Frenchman Bay towns. By 1820 the Frenchman Bay region launched about 2000 tons of shipping, competing with Penobscot Bay and midcoast ports (though dwarfed by Bath and Portland), and far exceeding any tonnage farther to the east.

The economic changes of the postwar era brought some slowly evolving trends in the social and political scene. Throughout Maine the Jeffersonian Democrats, especially in the Kennebec valley and back-country towns, began dominating local politics and sending their unruly representatives to a Massachusetts legislature still dominated by Federalists. After the war these Maine Democrats mounted a series of initiatives for statehood separate from Massachusetts, pointing to Boston's wartime indifference and failure to defend the east from the British. But such separatist efforts were stoutly resisted in the coastal towns, not only by landowners, but by all who counted on commercial ties and dependence on that "Coastwise Trade" law that uniquely enabled them to sell fish and timber, duty-free, to the west as far as New York. For these reasons Gouldsboro acted entirely typically, voting twice against early separation efforts.

Meanwhile the recovery era saw a continuation of earlier trends in religious affiliation as traditional Congregationalists associated with Massachusetts landowners were outnumbered almost two to one in the downeast area by the more fervent Baptists and Methodists. Gouldsboro followed Massachusetts law in raising a required "ministerial tax" to support the preaching of the gospel to its citizens, who were to be considered affiliated with one of the church denominations. Because there was no Congregational parish in Gouldsboro and apparently few adherents, a third of the town's ministerial tax was set aside in 1818 and 1819 for potential preaching for what was called "the Congregational party," but apparently no such preacher could be found. By 1820 these funds were apparently unused and reassigned to preaching by the local Baptist preacher, Job Chadwick. David Cobb's paternalistic Congregational ideology of the early 1800s had apparently never developed a lasting resonance with Gouldsboro townsmen.

The years 1819-1820 saw a much more fundamental departure for the coastal towns, as Maine's Democratic leader William King, elected to the Legislature, promoted a major change in the law for tariff duties. By the new law those early interstate tariffs were now almost eliminated for the Atlantic coast, opening up duty-free commerce for everyone. Suddenly Maine need no longer rely on its habitual economic tie, via the old duty-free "Coastwise trade" law, and had no need of its long dependence on the contiguous borders of Massachusetts. The resulting massive shift in political affiliation was really not so much a surprise, as a more a practical assessment—belated for some—of where their true interests lay. In the spring of 1819 the Maine state representatives went to the Massachusetts legislature, secured favorable terms for separation, and sent a referendum vote on separation and the new constitution to the towns in the summer of 1819. Now approximately two-thirds of the mostly coastal vote in the downeast counties came over in favor of separation. The Gouldsboro vote was totally transformed from former rejections: their voters now went for new statehood by a count of 47 to 2.

Thus did Gouldsboro voters finally acknowledge their true interests. In fall of 1819 the Maine towns elected 274 delegates to a convention to discuss a new state constitution, of which 236 supported separation and a constitution granting male suffrage without traditional property restrictions—nor any restrictions by race. When the new constitution went to town voters, only 14 turned out in Gouldsboro, though all were in favor. More surprising was the traditional vote for a new state governor and state senator: town selectman Sam Davis, General Cobb's son Henry, and clerk Nathan Shaw all threw in their hats, the latter two getting just one vote each, while a cautious majority actually voted for the new Jeffersonian Democrat, William King, as Maine's first Governor. Gouldsboro townsmen had finally opted for active regional self-determination, and a new role for themselves, however grudging, in the Federal Union.

The following year of 1820 General David Cobb retired as Bingham's land agent and permanently left Gouldsboro for his home in Taunton Massachusetts. In that year he wrote to his friend William Williamson with a backward-looking and disillusioned view of his years in Gouldsboro:

"The greater part of the inhabitants of the town follow lumbering and fishing, and like all other places where lumbering is persued, they are very intemperate, very lazy and very poor. It may be said in truth, altho' disgraceful to the town, that a majority of the inhabitants are drunkards."

--David Cobb to William D. Williamson, 1820 (quoted in Taylor).

Along with the rest of the downeast, Gouldsboro had outgrown its earlier dependence on its leading proprietors and large landowners and entered a new era of self-sufficient farming, commercial fishing, and increasingly active engagement with regional, state, and national politics. In March of 1820 all seven of Maine's new Congressmen voted *against* the "Missouri Compromise" bill granting Missouri slave status. Characteristically, Mainers stubbornly voted their independence, and also their consciences.

Sources

Banks, Ronald F. *Maine Becomes a State.* Middleton CT: Wesleyan, 1970.

Dallison, Robert L. *A Neighbourly War: New Brunswick and the War of 1812.* Frederickton NB: Goose Lane Press, 2012, pp 105-120.

Fraser, Robert. "The Battle of Hampden and Its Aftermath," in *Maine History* v. 43, 1, pp. 21-40 (January 2007) Portland ME 2007.

Greenan, John T. *Way Down East in Maine,* , pp. 115 ff. Morristown NJ (Compton Press) 1958. [Steuben history; account of Pigeon Hill battle].

Greenleaf, Moses. *Survey of Maine.* Augusta ME (Maine State Museum) reprint of edition of 1829.

Hornsby, Stephen et al. *Historical Atlas of Maine.* Orono ME (UME Press) 2015.

Johnson, Muriel S. *Early Families of Gouldsboro, Maine.* Rockport ME (Picton Press) 1990

Marini, Stephen A. "Religious Revolution in the District of Maine, 1780-1820," in Clark, Charles et al. Eds. *Maine in the Early Republic,* , pp. 118-145. Hanover NH (UPressNE) 1988.

O'Leary, Wayne M. *Maine Sea Fisheries*, Chapter 2, "The Role of Positive Government." Boston (Northeastern UP) 1996.

Savage, Richard M. II. "Discovery and Settlement of Mt. Desert," in *Mount Desert: An Informal History*, pp. 19-21. Gunnar Hansen Ed., Mount Desert ME 1989.

Smith, Joshua M. "Maine's Embargo Forts," in *Maine History* v.44: pp.143-154. Portland ME 2008.

Taylor, Alan. *Liberty Men and Great Proprietors.* Chapel Hill NC (UNC Press) 1990.

Town of Gouldsboro: *Town Records 1766-1895.* Rockland ME (Picton Press) DVD: 1990.

United States Census, Gouldsboro, Hancock County, Maine, 1790. 1800, 1810. [Accessed through Ancestry.com]

[Wood. Grace]. *Historical Researches of Gouldsboro Maine,* , pp. 17-55. Gouldsboro ME (Daughters of Liberty) 1904.

Young, George F.W. *The British Capture and Occupation of Downeast Maine, 1814-1815*, Stonington ME (Penobscot Books) 2014.

Appendix B

Gouldsboro's Founding Documents

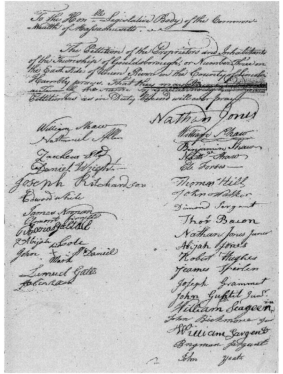

This townsmen's petition of 1789 accompanied a formal petition to the Massachusetts Legislature for incorporation as a self-governing township [see Document 1789]. It is signed by most of the leading Gouldsboro citizens, prominently led by proprietary founder Nathan Jones. [Massachusetts State Archive]

Document of January 1763

This early document of January, 1763, records the financial commitments of the three proprietors to the Commonwealth of Massachusetts, investing in the proportions that determined the final division of the Gouldsboro settlement into four quadrants. Here the three proprietors take up their shares from an attorney placeholder/petitioner who yields them their claims. Shaw and Gould with 45 of the 60 shares own three quarters or quadrants of the township, while Nathan Jones with 15 shares owns the other quadrant. After the financial upheavals of the Revolution, the Shaw and Gould three quadrants were surrendered to be bought by William Bingham, while Jones retained his original section, the northwest quadrant.

Acts of the Massachusetts General Court--Legislature

ORDER ACCEPTING REPORT OF COMMITTEE AND DIRECTING THE SECRETARY TO RECORD THE NAMES OF CERTAIN PERSONS AS GRANTEES OF LAND BETWEEN PENOBSCOT & ST.CROIX RIVERS.

The following report was presented by the Committee appointed for the purposes therein mentioned vizt [namely]

The Committee appointed to take bonds of the Petitioners for a grant of a Township of Land to Wait Wadsworth and others living at or near Duxborough, which Lands are lying between the Rivers Penobscot and St. Croix and called No. 3, in that division have attended that Service, and have taken sixty Bonds well executed for the sum of Fifty Pounds each of three persons vizt [namely]--

Twenty-two of Francis Shaw,   fifteen of Nathan Jones, and twenty-three of Robert Gould ;

who appeared to give such Bonds in the room of the Petitioners who refused and neglected to give said Bonds, agreeable to the conditions of said Grant, and have delivered the same to the Province Treasurer.

Which is humbly submitted   Gam. Bradford by order
Read and ordered That this Report be accepted, and the Secretary is hereby directed to record the names of the abovementioned Persons in the General Courts Books accordingly. *Passed January 27.*

Document of February 1763

With this Resolve of February 1763 the Massachusetts legislature confirmed ownership of the No. 3 sections to the three proprietors.

Acts of the Massachusetts General Court--Legislature

RESOLVE CONFIRMING LANID IN TOWNSHIP N° '3 TO DIVERS PERSONS-- THE SECRETARY went down to the House of Representatives on a Message from the Board with a Plan of Six Townships East of Penobscot, upon which was a Vote of the two Houses of the 26°' of January last confirming one of the said 'I'ownships viz' N° 3 to certain Persons therein mentioned, which Vote had not been signed by the Governor; and to propose that instead thereof a separate Vote might be passed for the same purpose, and laid before the Governor for his Consent. _ Upon Which the following Vote passed the whole Court Viz—

Resolued That the Lands described in a Township N° 3 in a plan of Six Townships Eastward of a River called Mount Desert River taken by order of this Court by Daniel Merrett and Mathew Austin Surveyors (including all Allowances therein made, and excepting all Islands therein described) that is to say from a certain Point at the bead of a small Cove, distant from another certain Point on the Eastern Side. of the said .Mount Desert River, in a course from the said River East 28 degrees South 12 miles and 140 Rods (which said Points shall hereafter be more exactly described and ascertained)to run by a Line North 28 degrees East 5 miles and three quarters, and from thence by a Line East 28 degrees South six miles, and from thence by a line South 28 degrees West to the Sea Coast, and from thence along the Sea Coast to the 'first mentioned Point—

S h a l l be granted so far as by this Court lawfully may be to Nathan Jones, Francis Shaw and Robert Gould and to their heirs and Assigns forever, the said Nathan, Francis and Robert having given Bonds to the Treasurer of this Province for the faithful fulfilling of the Conditions mentioned in the Grant of said Township, the original Grantees of said Wait

144

Wadsworth and others having refused to give Bonds according to the terms of the original Grant.

Provided the Lands described in said Township N° 3, do not exceed the Contents of six miles square with the usual Allowances of Swag of Chain, Water and mountains, and the whole remaining Subject nevertheless to all the conditions and reservations in the original Grant thereof made. *[Passed February 8, 1763]*

Document Sources

Acts and Resolves, Public and Private, of the Province of the Massachusetts Bay: to Which Are Prefixed The Charters of the Province, with Historical and Explanatory Notes and an Appendix. Vol. xvii, being a volume of the Appendix Containing Resolves, Etc, 1761-1764. Boston (Wright & Potter) 1910.

Commonwealth of Massachusetts State Archives. Acts of Incorporation. 1983

Document of January 1764

This lengthy Act of the Massachusetts legislature was the formal grant for all the numbered Townships to their respective proprietors, with full specifications for conditions of settlement. This included grants of land for schools and the ministry—some of which became public lots for the Gouldsboro town as later incorporated. There is a special extract for land specifications granted to Nathan Jones.

RESOLVE CONFIRMING THE GRANT OF SIX TOWNSHIPS EAST OF THE PENOBSCOT RIVER   [January 27, 1764]

WHEREAS their late Majesties King WILLIAM and QUEEN MARY, by their Letters Patent, bearing Date the seventh Day of October, in the third Year of their Reign, did Give and Grant unto the Inhabitants of the Province of the Massachusetts-Bay (among other Things) ail those Lands and Hereditaments, lying between the Territory of Nova-Scotia, and the River Sagadahock, then and ever since known and distinguished by the Name of the Territory of Sagadahock, together with all Islands lying within ten Leagues of the Main Land, within the said Bounds,

To HAVE AND TO HOLD the same unto the said Inhabitants and their Successors, to their own proper Use and Behoof for evermore. Provided always, That no Grant of Lands within the said Territory of Sagadahock made by the Governor and General Assembly of the said Province, should be of any Force or Effect, untill their Majesties, their Heirs. And Successors, should signify their Approbation of the same: * * * *s

And the said Governor, Council, and House of Representatives assembled as aforesaid, have also given and granted, and hereby do Give and Grant unto Nathan Jones, Francis Shaw, & Robert Gould; and their Associates and their Heirs, all that Tract of Land, adjoining to the Tract of Land beforementioned, and beginning at a Point on the West Side of a Creek marked K, ten Chains below the Falls, at N° 841 of the Survey, and running West seven Miles to mother Bay of the Sea, and from thence along the Sea Shore Easterly to the first Point, To HAVE AND TO HOLD the said Lands, with their Appurtenances, to them and their Heirs, to the only Use and Behoof of them and their Heirs forever, as Tenants in Common.

And the said Governor, Council, and House of Representatives assembled as aforesaid, have also given and granted, and hereby do Give and Grant unto Nathan Jones, Francis Shaw, & Robert Gould; and their Associates and their Heirs, all that Tract of Land, adjoining to the Tract of Land beforementioned, and beginning at a Point on the West Side of a Creek marked K, ten Chains below the Falls, at N° 841 of the Survey, and running West seven Miles to mother Bay of the Sea, and from thence along the Sea Shore Easterly to the first Point, To HAVE AND TO HOLD the said Lands, with their Appurtenances, to them and their Heirs, to the only Use and Behoof of them and their Heirs forever, as Tenants in Common.

[Provided that one fourth Part of the said Township shall be separated, and set apart unto the said Nathan Jones and his Associates in manner following,

A Line shall be run from the mouth of a Stream which falls from a large Pond, into the Bay next to N° Two, marked in the Plan D East by Compass unto the Bay in which Capt. Frost is settled; That the said Line be equally divided, and at the Point of the Division, another Line be run North by Compass to the bounding Line of the Township, on the North side, and South indefinitely; which Line shall be determined to the Southward by a Point from which a Line being run Westward, to the first mentioned Bay, may together with the said North and South Line. as to the East, and the said Bounding Line of the Township to the North, and the Shore of the said Bay to the West, Inclose one equal and equitable Fourth Part of the Township; Regard being had to the Quality as well as the Quantity of the. Land so Inclosed.

And Mr Jones, and Mr Frye the Surveyors heretofore employed in Surveying those Towns, shall run the said Lines, and determine the said south Boundary of the said Fourth Part as aforesaid; & shall make their Return upon Oath if the same shall be requir'd And if they cannot agree concerning the Settling and running the said South Line, they shall call in a third Person, by whose Arbitration the Thing shall be finally determined.

And the said Nathan Jones and his Associates shall do and perform one fourth Part of the Duties of the said Township.]

... RESERVING NEVERTHELESS, to be yielded and paid unto his Majesty, his Heirs and Successors, 'by the said several Grantees, and their respective Heirs and Assigns, one fifth Part of all Gold and Silver Oar and precious Stones, which shall hap· pen to be found, and gotten on the said Tracts of Land, or any of them, or any Part thereof. PROVIDED, that these Grants, or any of them, shall be of no Force or Effect, untill his Majesty, his Heirs and Successors, shall signify his or their Approbation thereof. And it is hereby provided and Declared, that the foregoing Grants, and each of them are and is made upon these express Considerations and Conditions, that the said several Grantees of the said several Tracts of Land hereafter to be made so many several Townships, and each of them shall within six Years after they shall have obtained his Majesty's approbation of such Grants, (unless prevented by War), settle each Township with SIXTY good PROTESTANT FAMILIES, and build sixty Houses, none to be less than EIGHTEEN Feet Square, or of equal Area, and seven Feet Stud; and clear and cultivate five Acres of Land on each Share, fit for Tillage, or Mowing; and that they build in each Township a suitable Meeting-House for the public Worship of God, and settle a learned PROTESTANT Minister, and make Provision for His comfortable and honourable Support. And that in each Township there be reserved and appropriated four whole Shares in the Division of the same (accounting one sixty fourth Part a Share) for the following Purposes, viz. one for the first settled or ordained minister, his Heirs and Assigns forever, one for the Use of the ministry, one to and for the Use of Harvard College in Cambridge, and one for the Use of a School forever. And if any of the Grantees or Proprietors, of any of the said Townships respectively, shall neglect, within the Term of six Years as afore· said, to do and perform the Conditions aforesaid, as shall respectively belong to his Share or Right as aforesaid, such Share or Right shall be entirely forfeited, and shall enure to the Use of this Province, this Grant or any Thing therein contained to the contrary notwithstanding.

PROVIDED NEVERTHELESS, that if the aforenamed Grantees, their Heirs and Assigns, shall not obtain his Majesty's Confirmation of these Grants before the Expiration of eighteen Months, to be computed from the Day of the Date hereof, then the said Grants, or such thereof as shall remain unconfirmed, shall cease and determine, and be null and void, this present Writing or any Thing therein contained to the contrary notwithstanding.

GIVEN in the Great and General Court, and Sealed with the public Seal of the Province the 27th of Jan" in the Fourth Year of the Reign of his Majesty GEORGE the Third, by the GRACE OF GOD, of Great-Britain, France and Ireland, King, Defender of the Faith &c. and in the Year of our Lord One Thousand Seven Hundred and Sixty four.

Document of May 1787

*In the uncertain year of 1787, with the drafts of the new national Constitution being debated as replacement to the old Confederation, and eastern Maine still in the County of Lincoln, competing petitions were submitted to the Massachusetts Legislature about incorporating Gouldsboro as a new town with power to tax and be taxed. This "naysayers" petition, which prevailed, is interesting for calling upon the authority a Town Meeting when the settlement had as yet no formal Town status, buts yet citing the fragile state of the community as unready for Town status in unstable times. Note that the colonial settlement granted in the 1760s to the three Proprietors, though it was designated by the term "**Township**," nevertheless **had no formal authority** as an incorporated Town to govern its inhabitants, to pass town ordinances, or to raise taxes.*

To the Honorable Legislative Body of the Commonwealth of Massachusetts.

The Petition of the Freeholders, Inhabitants of the Township of Gouldsboro or Number three on the East side of Union River, the County of Lincoln.

Humbly shews [shows]—

That whereas there was a Petition for the Incorporation of this Township sent to the General Court, [dated March 7, 1787], a copy of which we have received with an order of the Court thereon to shew cause if any we have why this Township shall not be incorporated;

Said order of Court has this day been acted upon, **at a legal Town Meeting**, and we beg leave to shew the following Reasons why this Township shall not be Incorporated. *Viz t [videlicet –* "namely"] --

That there is but Twenty seven Settled Families within the Bounds of this Township, and the greater part of them so poor, that it is with extreme Difficulty they can make a bear existence the Year Round; Therefore unable to pay taxes;

And as to the former Petition, -- that but very few of the proper settlers of this Township had any knowledge of it until after it was put in execution, and that the greater part of the Signers of said Petition are single men, some of which are no way likely to settle here, some not of Lawful Age, and some of their Names has never been known to have lived here; the signing of said Petition having been carried on without the Consideration and Regulation of a Town Meeting.

The Petitioners beg leave to inform that they have not received the order of the Court until the twenty seventh of May instant.

The Petitioners beg leave to add that the foregoing is a True Representation, and humbly Relys on the Virtue of our Legislature, that they will consider our Inability, and Post Pone our incorporation until better fitted for it, and we in duty bound will ever pray.

Dated at Gouldboro 28th May 1787 ···Signer names ...

| James Noonan | Benjamin Godfrey | Samuel Libby |

Thomas Hill —·· Committee

| Jonathan Tracy jr | Joel Moore | Asa Tracy | ?? Tibbetts |

| John McDaniel X his mark | Clement Fernald | Samuel Joy |

| Phineas Whitten | Jonathan Tracy sr | John Gubtail |

| Jos? Perry | Benjamin Lusk[?] | Noah Young | John Gubtail jr |

| Joseph Newman | John Bickmore | William Sargent |

Benj Allen [_ _ _ _ Illegible]

Document of February 1789

Gouldsboro's successful petition for Town incorporation coincided with the Massachusetts Legislature's action to recognize a large group of eastern Townships for incorporation in February of 1789. Here the petitioners presented a draft of what they expected to be their act of incorporation. Promptly after incorporation a group of the new towns of eastern Maine were shifted from the original Lincoln County into the new Hancock County. Here is reprinted part of what was a handwritten draft—possibly by a clerk?-- of the formal act of incorporation. It is undated but has a notation added as "Passed Febr 17, 1789." Note that the Town's name in this handwritten petition was regularly spelled "Goldsboro" or "Goldsborough." Below are transcribed the opening sentences of the handwritten draft.

Commonwealth of Massachusetts In the Year of our LORD One Thousand Seven hundred eighty nine.

In an Act for Incorporating The Planation of Goldsboro—so called in the County of Lincoln into a Town by the name of Goldsboro.

Whereas it appears to this court that the inhabitants of the Plantation called Goldsborough Labour under many Inconveniences in their present unincorporated state.

Be it enacted by the Senate and House of Representatives in General Court assembled and by the Authority of the same;

That the Plantation of Goldsboro ["ough" is crossed out] and included within the boundaries hereafter described, together with the inhabitants thereof--
     Be and hereafter are Incorporated Into a Town by the name of Goldsborough.....

The rest of the handwritten draft is the complete legal text of the formal act of incorporation as passed in the Legislature. That complete and detailed text can be found in previously published form as it appears on pages 17-18 of "Historical Researches of Gouldsboro Maine." [Grace Wood Clark, ed., Gouldsboro Maine 1904.]

Accompanying the handwritten draft for the act of incorporation was a Petition urging its passage—reproduced in facsimile at the beginning of this Appendix. It was signed by many of the early worthies of the new town. The Petition regularly spelled the Town's name "Gouldsborough."

To the Hon-ble Legislative Body of the Commonwealth of Massachusetts----

The Petition of the Proprietors and Inhabitants of the Township of Gouldsborough, or Number Three on the East side of Union River in the County of Lincoln;

Humbly prays—That they may be Incorporated into a Town by the name of Gouldsborough; and your Petttioners as in Duty bound will ever pray.

Nathan Jones   William Shaw Benjamin Shaw

Nathanl Shaw Eli Forbes   Thomas Hill   John Walker

Dimon Sergant   Thos Bacon   Nathan Jones jr   Abijah Jones

Robert Hughes   James Spirlin   Joseph Grammet

John Gubtail jr   William Seageen   John Bickmore jr

William Sergent   Benjamin Sergant   John Yeats

William Shaw [2nd?]   Nathaniel Allen   Tadheus Shed

Daniel Wright   Joseph Richardson   Edward White

James Noonan   Clement Fernald   Thomas Gubtail

Abijah Cole   John Daniel [X mark]   Lemuel Gates

Peter Clark [?]

Index